FIRST IN A SERIES OF  CROCKETT'S CORNER

WHEAT COOKIN' MADE EASY

By: Pam Crockett

Cover Photo by: Scott Smith Photography
                        Orem, Utah

Layout by: Kent A. Woodruff

Inside artwork by: Sandy Phelps
                        Kristen Phelps
                        Shelly Verhaal

Davy the Raccoon "Logo" created by Kristen Phelps

Editing by: Lonnie Crockett

Compiled by: Pam Crockett
                        Sandy Phelps

Printed in the United States

1st Printing © 2002

ISBN# 0-9717696-0-5

Copyright © 2002 by Crockett's Corner

DMT Publishing
900 North 400 West #12
North Salt Lake, Utah
(801) 397-1826

INTRODUCTION

How many of you have wheat stored away? How many of you use the wheat that is being stored away? Well, I have an interesting story to tell you about how this cookbook came to be.

It all started in the summer of 1999 when my husband found a fantastic buy on some organic hard red wheat from a farmer in Idaho. The only problem was, we had to buy 10,000 #'s of the stuff. That was O.K.; my husband thought he could sell much of it to our friends and family members. He got it at such a great buy you see. The day came when the farmer delivered it. WOW! Do you know how much space 10,000 #'s of wheat occupies? Well, it took up the space in our garage where my car used to be parked. That too was O.K.; my husband said it wouldn't be there long. Well, it did sit for about a month. You see, everybody we know has wheat stored. Interestingly enough, nobody used it. It just sat there in their food storage.

Back to the wheat in my garage. It sat there in 75-pound sacks and believe me there were many of them. I became concerned that mice might get into it, so we decided we better start canning it. Well, all the canneries were booked solid for the next several months here in Utah. So, we started looking for a home canner and ordered one hot off the assembly line here in Salt Lake City. We went down and picked it up and brought it home. We also had to get some pallets full of the #10 sized cans. Say, 1,500 or so. Trying to get into the mode of this being a fun family activity we started in, but where do we put all these cans? We already had our food storage room packed, so my husband had to have a cellar built in back of our home to store all this canned wheat.

What do I do with all this wheat? I bought books on wheat and started studying up on all the different things one can do with it. I got excited and found out there are so many different things one can do with wheat. I was later asked to teach a class on "Cooking with Wheat" at a church function and it turned out to be a hit. Everyone in attendance was excited to try a new recipe. From then on, I was asked to teach in different directions and many would come up to me and say I should compile all of these easy and fun recipes into a cookbook. So guess what? This is the first cookbook in a series of cookbooks soon to be published. Thanks to my impulsive husband and his wonderful attitude about being prepared, this book has come to be.

Pam Crockett

DEDICATION

To families out there who have wheat in their food storage. Bless you for being prepared. May you have fun learning new ideas with your wheat and please, eat what you store and store what you eat.

APPRECIATION

To all of my dear friends and family members who took the time out of their busy schedules to share a special recipe or favorite dish.

A heartfelt thanks goes out to my patient husband Lonnie, my oldest daughter Shelly, Kristen Phelps and my dear friend Sandy Phelps, who helped me compile and piece this all together.

COMPILATION

This cookbook is a collection of recipes that have been gathered from many sources. All the recipes in this book have wheat included, whether it be sprouted, ground, boiled, baked, fried, ect……..

NOTICE: Information in this book is true and complete to the best of our knowledge. However, the author and publisher disclaim all liability incurred in connection with the use of information appearing in this book.

SOME KNOWLEDGE ABOUT WHEAT

WHEAT: A cereal plant of the grass family is a major food and an important commodity of the world. The plant is an annual that grows best where the weather is cool during its early growth. Modern varieties are usually classified as winter wheats and spring wheats. Hard-kerneled varieties yield flour with a high gluten content, used to make breads; soft-kerneled varieties are starchier, and their flour is used to make cakes and biscuits. The hardest –kerneled wheat is durum; its flour is used in the manufacture of macaroni, spaghetti, and other pasta products. Wheat is also used in the manufacturing of whiskey and beer. The bran (the residue from milling the wheat grain), and the vegetative plant parts make valuable livestock feed. Wheat was one of the first grains to be cultivated. Bread wheat was grown in the Nile River valley by 5000 B.C.

Wheat should be the first choice when considering the storage of grains. It is easy to store and has high nutritive value. It is very rich in protein, iron, niacin, calcium, thiamin, riboflavin as well as vitamins E and B. When sprouted, it also supplies vitamins A and C, which would help you maintain your health if you had little or no fresh fruit or vegetables available in your diet.
Whole-wheat flour is the foundation of good bread making. It contains the highest amount of gluten of any grain. This becomes the elastic part of the dough and holds the yeast bubbles within the bread causing the bread to rise. The gluten in wheat is the only gluten that can be removed from the rest of the grain. High protein wheat (Hard Red) is best for making breads and gluten. (Soft) wheat can be used in many other preparations such as: snacks, cereals, crackers, muffins, soups, and even sprouting.

Choose wheat carefully for storage purposes. Select a hard winter or hard spring wheat with a protein count of 14% or above. Moisture content is extremely important as well. It is recommended that the moisture content be 10% or less. Insects are unable to reproduce in clean grain with low moisture content. Wheat will store indefinitely if properly stored in a cool, dry place.

The most convenient way to grind your wheat is with a wheat grinder or grain mill. You can grind wheat into flour or crack it for cereal using either piece of equipment. Whole-wheat flour does not store like white flour very well. If possible, grind wheat just before using it to retain its full nutrition. The nutrients are quickly reduced or lost after grinding and left on the shelf.

Introduce whole-wheat foods to your family a little at a time.

DID YOU KNOW YOU CAN SPROUT WHEAT?

General Directions

Sprouting is one of the fastest ways of improving the nutritional value of foods.
You can sprout many grains and seeds, but we are only going to talk about sprouting wheat and the different ways in which you can do it.

When wheat is sprouted, it softens the outside of the kernel so it is easier to eat. It also, increases the nutrients and vitamins in the wheat. After the wheat has sprouted it is now considered a fresh vegetable.

You can sprout wheat in a quart jar, a sprout bag, a pyrex dish, a basket, or they have commercial sprouters one can purchase.

Place a 3 T. to ¼ C. of wheat in a quart jar.
Cover with lukewarm water. Let soak 8 – 12 hours.
Place cheesecloth, nylon or light screen on top of jar and tighten down with ring.
Drain water off, (you may save the water for cooking or plants) rinse & drain again.
Lay jar on side and place in a dark warm cupboard.
Rinse two or three times daily, and be sure to drain well.
The wheat should sprout in 2-3 days.
When small sprouts begin to show, rinse, drain and store in the refrigerator in a closed container
Wheat sprouts should be harvested before the first leaves are fully developed and the root is only as long as the seed. Otherwise, they will become tough.

You can use sprouted wheat in your salads, on sandwiches, in soups, breads and main dishes. Growing sprouts is like having an indoor garden all year round and they taste delicious!

NOW GO TRY IT AND HAVE FUN !

Wheat Grass – Preparing & Growing

This is a subject I will just touch upon. There are books available that go into great detail about the uses of Wheat Grass.

Place about 1" of potting soil on a plastic seed tray that has drainage in the bottom. Place wheat seeds that have been soaked and sprouted into this soil. Water the tray, place a protective cover over it and set aside for a few days. Uncover, water and place in indirect light. Keep moist and watch it grow. Just like a "Chia Pet". For juicing, let the grass grow until it is 8 – 10 inches long. Then cut, wash and prepare to juice. There are several commercial juicers available, either hand or motorized that can be purchased.

WHAT IS BULGUR ?

Bulgur is just whole kernel wheat berries that have been precooked for easier and quicker use later. It is not difficult to prepare. When they are cooked, they are slightly chewy and sweet.

Bulgur resembles rice and is used like rice in the Middle East as a delicious golden pilaf. It is becoming more and more popular in the U.S.A. One thing that makes bulgur so appealing is that, because it's already been partially cooked, it cooks quickly. Many people find its fluffiness appealing. In fact, you can use bulgur in place of rice for most recipes. You'll get a nutrition bonus if you do.

Coarse bulgur is usually used to make pilaf or stuffing. Medium ground bulgur is often used in cereals. The finest grind of bulgur is especially suited to the popular cold Middle Eastern salad called tabbouleh (recipe under salads).

Bulgur lends its nutty flavor to whatever it is combined with. Perhaps one of bulgurs most useful roles is as a meat extender. It will blend in well, without being obvious and without disintegrating into mush. Add some extra liquid if you are using very lean meat.

FOLLOW THE RECIPE

1. Wash wheat in cool water and discard water.
2. Place wheat in medium saucepan, add enough water to cover wheat (about 2 inches)
3. Bring to boil. Turn off heat, and let rest 1-2 hrs.
4. Drain excess water & spread wheat thinly on cookie sheet or shallow pan & dry in oven at 200 degrees, until very dry, so it will crack easily.
5. Wet surface of dried wheat slightly & rub kernels between hands to loosen & remove chaff.
6. Crack wheat in moderate size pieces, using a mill, grinder or mortar and pestle. In some cases the wheat may be used whole, giving a very chewy product.
7. Store in airtight container on shelf.
8. This processed bulgur, when thoroughly dried, is easily stored and may be used in many wheat recipes. If the recipe calls for cooked wheat or bulgur, simply boil in water for 5 to 10 minutes, and it will double in volume. (1-cup bulgur to 2 cups water). Otherwise, there is no need to cook it again.

WHAT IS GLUTEN?

You can go through a process to make raw gluten at home, or you can buy the commercial product sold in stores called "Wheat Gluten Flour". I will quickly explain what it is and what it is used for:

Gluten is the sticky substance in wheat which traps bubbles of carbon dioxide that form when the yeast "feeds" on sugars in the dough. Gluten holds the gas bubbles, causing the dough to rise. Kneading causes gluten.

Gluten is a type of vegetable protein that needs to be supplemented with another protein: such as eggs, milk, nuts, meat, soy, cheese, etc.

Gluten is easily digested and because of the tender texture, it makes a wonderful substitute for meats. Gluten is a delicious vegetarian alternative because it is made from the protein of wheat. Hence, wherever meat is used in a recipe, use gluten.

When gluten is separated from the rest of the wheat kernel, it is quite tasteless. Therefore, a flavor needs to be added. By adding a meat broth, a meat flavor is placed in the gluten and it can be combined with meat in a meat recipe or it can be used alone as a meat substitute.

The gluten in the wheat kernel is quite unique in which you can separate it from the starchy part of the grain. In other grains such as rye, barley, maize, etc. this extraction cannot be done.

Gluten is separated from the starchy part of the kernel by washing the starch away under running water. You can take a ball of flour (which has already had water added to it) and soak it overnight in a bowl of water or you can mix the flour and water in a mixer for 10 minutes.

The process of making gluten should only take you about 15 minutes. Unless you like the idea of the overnight soaking. However, that process tends to wash away a lot of the vitamins.

There are many good books out there on the subject of "Gluten", so I will just give you (1) simple recipe on how it is made.

A QUICK EASY METHOD FOR MAKING GLUTEN

7 Cups Whole Wheat Flour
3 cups cool water

Add water to whole-wheat flour and knead well. It will form into a ball. Place that ball in the bowl under water and knead some more. As you are kneading the gluten is extracted. Hold the dough under the cool water, working with your hands, wash until the water runs clear. The gluten should look like a grayish type bubble gum. This process shouldn't take longer than 15 minutes.
Knead a package of dry onion soup mix into the ball of gluten. Form the raw gluten into a long skinny roll while using wet hands. Slice into mini steaks and place pieces on a greased, floured cookie sheet. Dry in oven at 250 degrees for 1 – 1½ hours or until dry. Use these pieces in soups or stews. They can be frozen until ready to use.

You can also slice the above gluten ball into small steaks and put directly into a seasoned meat broth and simmer for 30 minutes. Press out as much of the liquid as possible and even blot with a paper towel. Place pieces on a greased, lightly floured cookie sheet and bake at 350 degrees, turning once for 30 minutes. Store these steaks in the refrigerator. They will be more moist than the steaks that have been dried and they can be used immediately.

Beef Flavored Gluten

2 cups water   ¼ cup dried onions
2 Tbsp. beef base granules   ¼ Tbsp. pepper
1 Tbsp. soy sauce   4 tsp. seasoned salt

Add all above ingredients to water and bring to a boil. Add above pieces of gluten and simmer for about 30 minutes.

Chicken Flavored Gluten

WHEAT

2 cups water   2 tsp. poultry seasoning
2 Tbsp. chicken base granules or   ½ tsp. onion powder
chicken bouillon cubes   ½ tsp. salt

Add all above ingredients to water and bring to a boil. Add gluten pieces and simmer for about 30 minutes. Remove gluten from water and allow to dry.

TABLE OF CONTENTS

Bread & Biscuit Corner

Aunt Thelma's Bible Bread

3 ½ cups whole wheat flour
2 Tbsp. olive oil
1 Tbsp. honey
½ tsp. salt
1 ½ cup warm milk
1 egg

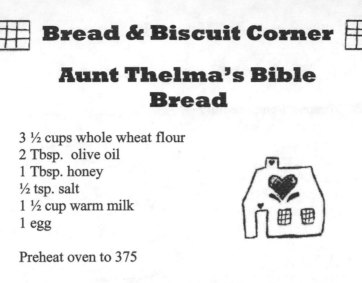

Preheat oven to 375

In a large mixing bowl, combine all ingredients and blend well. Turn out on a floured surface and knead for 5 minutes. Divide in half. Roll into flat 10-inch circles. Bake on lightly greased pizza pans for 20 minutes. Cool on a wire rack.

Serve with butter and jam.

From a friend:

Baked Brown Bread

1 ½ cups all-purpose flour
2 ½ tsp. baking soda
1 ½ tsp. salt
¼ cup sugar
2 cups whole wheat flour
1/3 cup vegetable shortening
1 egg, beaten
2 cups buttermilk
¾ molasses
1 cup raisins

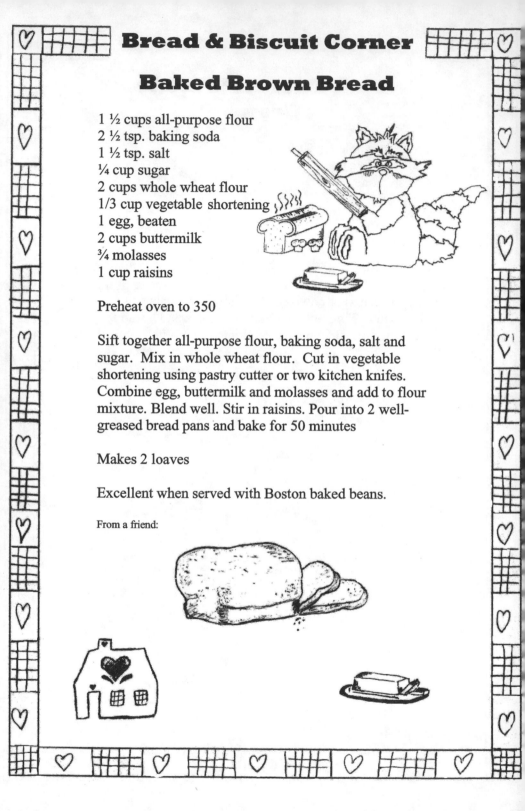

Preheat oven to 350

Sift together all-purpose flour, baking soda, salt and sugar. Mix in whole wheat flour. Cut in vegetable shortening using pastry cutter or two kitchen knifes. Combine egg, buttermilk and molasses and add to flour mixture. Blend well. Stir in raisins. Pour into 2 well-greased bread pans and bake for 50 minutes

Makes 2 loaves

Excellent when served with Boston baked beans.

From a friend:

Bread & Biscuit Corner

Bread Sticks Made Easy
(No yeast)

4 cups whole-wheat flour
1 Tbsp. salt
¼ cup powder milk
1-cup water
½ cup vegetable oil
3 Tbsp. honey

Preheat oven to 375

Mix dry ingredients together with wooden spoon. Add water, vegetable oil and honey. Blend mixture well and turn out onto a floured surface. Knead for 5 minutes. Pinch off a golf ball sized piece and roll with palm of hands to form a 3-inch stick. Roll in sesame seed is desired.

Bake on a sprayed cookie sheet for about 20 minutes. Brush immediately with butter. You may also sprinkle on some garlic or seasoned salt for a little zing.

From a dear friend: Sandy Phelps

Crunchy French Bread

2 cup whole wheat flour
2 Tbsp. dry yeast
2 Tbsp. sugar
1 egg
2 Tbsp. butter flavored shortening
1 tsp. salt
2 cups very warm water
4 cups all-purpose flour

In mixer bowl, blend together first six ingredients. Add warm water and mix well. Beat on high speed for 2 minutes. Let dough rest for 10 minutes. Add the rest of the flour and knead with dough hook for 10 minutes or by hand for 15 minutes.

Shape into 2 small or one large loaf and make small slices diagonally across top of loaves. Allow to rise until doubled.

Sprinkle greased baking sheet with cornmeal to prevent loaves from sticking. Place a shallow pan of water on the bottom rack in oven. Bake loaves on middle rack at 425 degrees for 15 minutes. Lower temperature to 375 and continue baking for 10 to 15 minutes or until bread sounds hollow when tapped on the top and it is lightly golden brown.

This recipe also makes great pizza crust. Will make 2 large pizzas.

From a friend:

Bread & Biscuit Corner

Dairy Free Whole Wheat Bread

5 ½ cups warm water
½ cup vegetable oil
3 Tbsp. instant yeast
½ cup honey
10-11 cup whole wheat flour
1½ Tbsp. salt

Mix warm water, vegetable oil, yeast, honey and 7 cups whole wheat flour. Blend well and let dough rest 10 minutes to proof the yeast. Add salt and 3 to 4 cups more whole wheat flour until good kneading consistency. Turn out on floured surface and knead for 10 minutes. Let rise for 1 hour. Punch down and shape into 5 or 6 loaves. Place in well-greased bread pans. Let rise until doubled. Bake at 350 degrees for 30 to 35 minutes. Remove from pans and cool on rack.

Makes 5-6 loaves

From a friend:

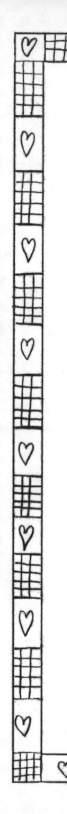

Bread & Biscuit Corner

Delicious Indian Fried Bread

2 cups whole wheat flour
1 Tbsp. baking powder
¼ cup powdered milk
1 tsp. salt
1 cup warm water
2 cups vegetable oil

Place all ingredients except vegetable oil in a large mixing bowl and stir just until blended. Divide into 2" balls and roll into ¼" thick circles. Cut each circle into 6 wedges. Pour vegetable oil into a deep frying pan and heat to 375 degrees. Fry wedges until crisp. Place on paper towels to drain. Sprinkle immediately with cinnamon and sugar or serve with butter, peanut butter, honey or jam.

To serve with main dish, sprinkle with Parmesan cheese or serve with herb butter.

8

Bread & Biscuit Corner

Delicious Whole Wheat Bread

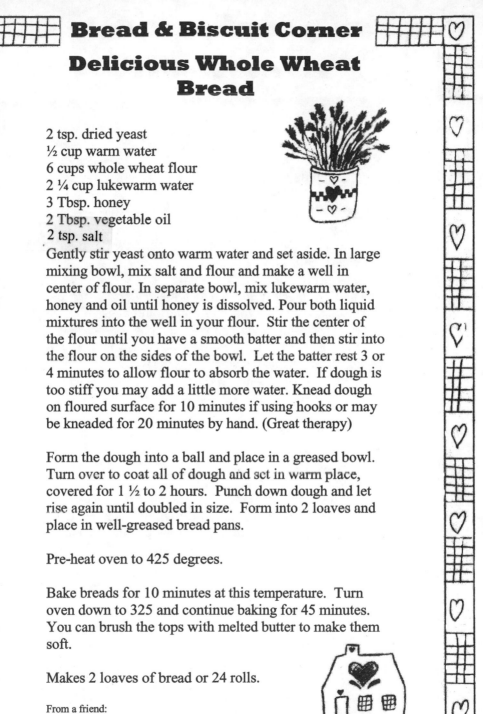

2 tsp. dried yeast
½ cup warm water
6 cups whole wheat flour
2 ¼ cup lukewarm water
3 Tbsp. honey
2 Tbsp. vegetable oil
2 tsp. salt

Gently stir yeast onto warm water and set aside. In large mixing bowl, mix salt and flour and make a well in center of flour. In separate bowl, mix lukewarm water, honey and oil until honey is dissolved. Pour both liquid mixtures into the well in your flour. Stir the center of the flour until you have a smooth batter and then stir into the flour on the sides of the bowl. Let the batter rest 3 or 4 minutes to allow flour to absorb the water. If dough is too stiff you may add a little more water. Knead dough on floured surface for 10 minutes if using hooks or may be kneaded for 20 minutes by hand. (Great therapy)

Form the dough into a ball and place in a greased bowl. Turn over to coat all of dough and set in warm place, covered for 1 ½ to 2 hours. Punch down dough and let rise again until doubled in size. Form into 2 loaves and place in well-greased bread pans.

Pre-heat oven to 425 degrees.

Bake breads for 10 minutes at this temperature. Turn oven down to 325 and continue baking for 45 minutes. You can brush the tops with melted butter to make them soft.

Makes 2 loaves of bread or 24 rolls.

From a friend:

Fried Scones

2 pkgs. Yeast
¾ cups warm water
2 Tbsp. sugar
3¼ cups warm buttermilk
2 eggs, slightly beaten
6 tbsp. vegetable oil
1 Tbsp. salt
3 tsp. baking powder
½ tsp. baking soda
7-8 cups whole wheat

In small bowl, gently stir together yeast, warm water and sugar. Set aside. Mix together buttermilk, eggs, vegetable oil, salt, baking powder and baking soda. Blend well. Add 7 cups whole wheat flour and mix until dough is soft and leaves side of bowl. (Add more flour if needed) Cover bowl and let rise for one hour. Punch down and refrigerate for 6 hours.

Remove from refrigerator 10 minutes before using. Knead slightly on floured surface and roll out to ½ inch thick. Tear off desired size pieces and fry in 1 inch of hot vegetable oil. Drain on paper towels and serve hot with butter and sprinkle with powdered sugar. Also great served with honey butter. Dough will stay good in refrigerator for up to 10 days. Tear off just the amount you need and keep the rest refrigerated.

From a friend:

A Favorite !

Havurah Hallah

Braided bread

2 pkgs. dry yeast	4 ½ to 5 cups whole wheat
½ cup warm water	pastry flour
¾ cup milk	2 eggs + 1 egg yolk
¼ cup butter or margarine	
2 Tbsp. sugar	1 Tbsp. water
2 tsp. salt	1 Tbsp. sesame or poppy seeds

Soften yeast in warm water. Warm butter, milk, sugar and salt in sauce pan until sugar dissolves. Cool to lukewarm. Stir in 2 cups flour and beat well. Add yeast mixture, 2 eggs and beat again. Stir in enough flour to make a soft dough. Turn out on lightly floured surface and knead for 8 to 10 minutes. Place in greased bowl, turn once and cover. Let rise, in a warm place, until doubled in size. Punch down; divide into three equal pieces and roll into balls. Cover and let rest for 10 minutes. With floured hand, roll each ball of dough into an 18-inch rope. Braid ropes together and tuck in ends. Beat egg yolk with 1 Tbsp. water and brush braid. Sprinkle with sesame or poppy seeds and place on greased baking sheet. Bake for 45 to 50 minutes at 375 degrees.

From a friend:

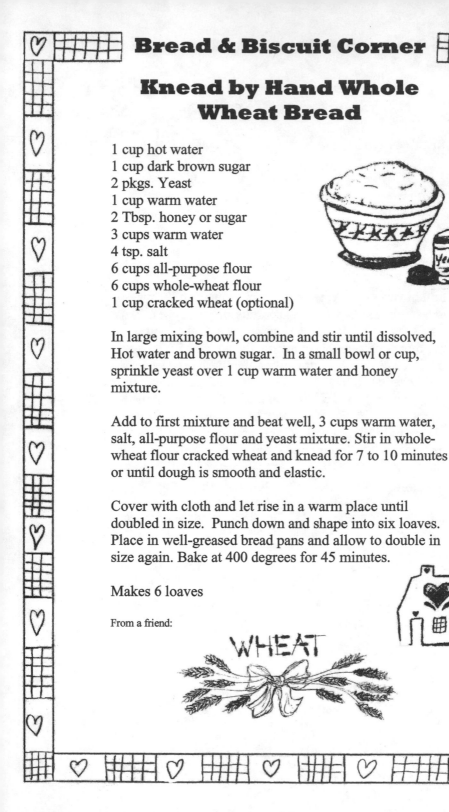

Knead by Hand Whole Wheat Bread

1 cup hot water
1 cup dark brown sugar
2 pkgs. Yeast
1 cup warm water
2 Tbsp. honey or sugar
3 cups warm water
4 tsp. salt
6 cups all-purpose flour
6 cups whole-wheat flour
1 cup cracked wheat (optional)

In large mixing bowl, combine and stir until dissolved, Hot water and brown sugar. In a small bowl or cup, sprinkle yeast over 1 cup warm water and honey mixture.

Add to first mixture and beat well, 3 cups warm water, salt, all-purpose flour and yeast mixture. Stir in whole-wheat flour cracked wheat and knead for 7 to 10 minutes or until dough is smooth and elastic.

Cover with cloth and let rise in a warm place until doubled in size. Punch down and shape into six loaves. Place in well-greased bread pans and allow to double in size again. Bake at 400 degrees for 45 minutes.

Makes 6 loaves

From a friend:

WHEAT

Bread & Biscuit Corner

Molasses Whole Wheat Bread

2½ cups milk
½ cup butter + 1 Tbsp. <u>or</u> margarine
¾ cup molasses
½ cup honey
1 Tbsp. + 2 tsp. salt
2 cups warm water
2½ Tbsp. yeast
4 eggs, slightly beaten
11-12 cups whole-wheat flour
2-3 cups all-purpose flour

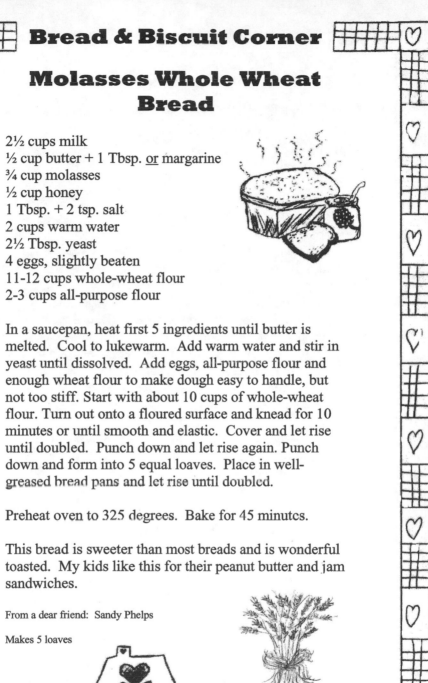

In a saucepan, heat first 5 ingredients until butter is melted. Cool to lukewarm. Add warm water and stir in yeast until dissolved. Add eggs, all-purpose flour and enough wheat flour to make dough easy to handle, but not too stiff. Start with about 10 cups of whole-wheat flour. Turn out onto a floured surface and knead for 10 minutes or until smooth and elastic. Cover and let rise until doubled. Punch down and let rise again. Punch down and form into 5 equal loaves. Place in well-greased bread pans and let rise until doubled.

Preheat oven to 325 degrees. Bake for 45 minutes.

This bread is sweeter than most breads and is wonderful toasted. My kids like this for their peanut butter and jam sandwiches.

From a dear friend: Sandy Phelps

Makes 5 loaves

Bread & Biscuit Corner

Old Fashioned Bread

1 cup milk, scalded
½ cup vegetable shortening
½ cup sugar
1 Tbsp. salt
1 cup cold water
1 yeast cake
1/3 cup lukewarm water
1 Tbsp. sugar
2 cups whole wheat
5 cups all- purpose flour

In large mixing bowl add scalded milk, vegetable shortening, sugar, salt and cold water. Dissolve yeast in lukewarm water and add sugar. Add milk and yeast mixture together. Add flours and blend well. Knead for 8 to 10 minutes until dough becomes smooth and elastic. Put into greased bowl in warm place and let rise until doubled. (About 1 hour)

Punch dough down and divide in half. Shape into two loaves and put into greased bread pans and let rise until double in size. Bake for 40 to 45 minutes at 350 degrees.

From a friend:

Old Fashioned Corn Bread

1 cup whole-wheat flour
1 cup cornmeal
1 tsp. salt
1 tsp. baking powder
¾ tsp. baking soda
2 eggs, lightly beaten
1 ½ cups buttermilk
2 ½ Tbsp. olive oil

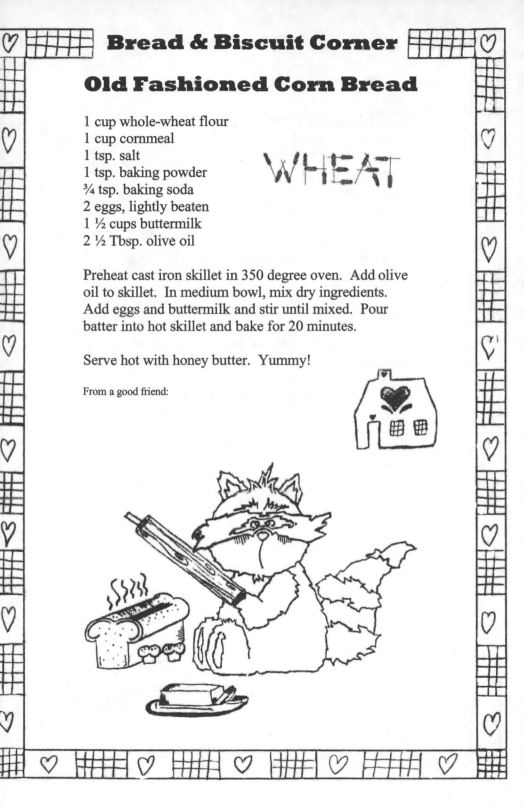

Preheat cast iron skillet in 350 degree oven. Add olive oil to skillet. In medium bowl, mix dry ingredients. Add eggs and buttermilk and stir until mixed. Pour batter into hot skillet and bake for 20 minutes.

Serve hot with honey butter. Yummy!

From a good friend:

Potato Wheat Bread

6 cups hot tap water
2/3 cup vegetable oil
2/3 cup honey
3 Tbsp. salt
2 eggs, slightly beaten
2/3 cup powdered milk mixed with 1cup whole wheat flour
¾ cup potato flakes
12-13 cups whole wheat flour
2 pkgs. Yeast

Preheat oven to 400 degrees

Combine in mixer bowl: hot water, vegetable oil, honey, salt, eggs, milk mixture, potato flakes and 7 cups of whole wheat flour. Mix well. Add yeast and mix well. Add 6 or 7 more cups of whole wheat flour and knead on low for 10 minutes or by hand for 15 minutes.

Form into four equal loaves, place in oiled bread pans and let rise until doubled. Bake for 15 minutes at 400 degrees, lower temperature to 350 degrees and bake another 30 minutes. This gives the bread a wonderful crispy crust.

From a dear friend: Sue Marlowe

Quick & Easy Thirty
Minute Hamburger Buns

3½ cups warm tap water
¾ cup sugar
1 cup vegetable oil
6 Tbsp. yeast
1 Tbsp. salt
2 eggs, slightly beaten
10½ cups whole wheat flour

Combine water, sugar, vegetable oil and yeast. Mix well
and set aside for 15 minutes. Preheat oven to 425
degrees. Add remaining ingredients to yeast mixture
and mix well. Shape into rolls or hamburger buns.
Place on a greased cookie sheet, about 12 to a sheet and
let rise for 10 to 12 minutes. Bake for 10 minutes or
until lightly golden brown.

This dough is perfect for quick cinnamon or caramel nut
rolls also.

From a friend:

WHEAT

Bread & Biscuit Corner

Simple and Quick Wheat Soy Bread

2½ cups whole wheat
½ cup + 2 Tbsp. soy flour
2 tsp. baking soda
½ tsp. salt
2 cups buttermilk
2 Tbsp. vegetable oil
¼ cup honey.

In large bowl, stir together dry ingredients. Blend liquid ingredients and add to dry ingredients. It is important that you blend this batter very well. Pour into well greased bread pan and bake at 325 degrees for about 1 hour or until a toothpick comes out clean.

Makes 1 loaf

From a friend:

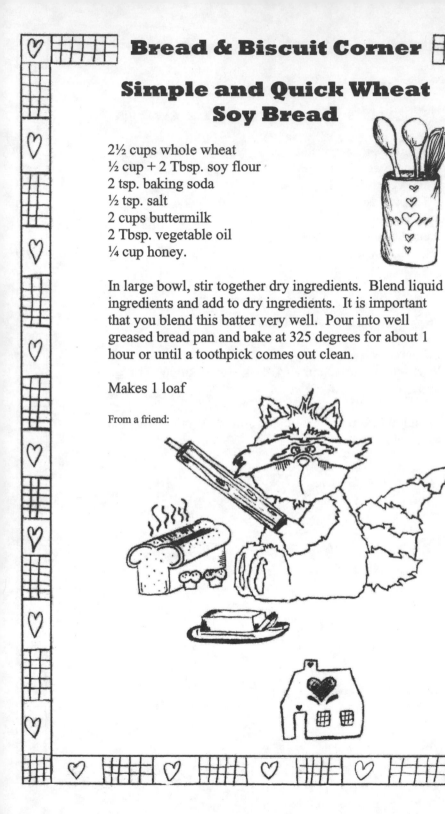

18

Sprouted Whole Wheat Bread

1 cup milk, scalded
½ cup water
2 Tbsp. vegetable oil
2 Tbsp. honey
1 egg
1 cup sprouts
1 tsp. salt
1 pkg. dry yeast
4 cups whole wheat flour

Liquefy in blender, scalded milk, water, vegetable oil, honey, egg and sprouts. Pour into large mixing bowl and add salt and 2 cups of whole wheat flour. Mix well. Add yeast and remaining 2 cups of flour. Knead for 10 minutes. Form into a greased 5" by 9" bread pan and let rise until doubled in bulk. Bake for 60 to 70 minutes at 350 degrees.

Makes 1 loaf

From a friend:

A Favorite !

Wheat Berry Bread

1 cup cooked wheat berries (see breakfast section)
2 cups warm water
¼ cup honey
1 pkg. yeast
2 tsp. salt
1/3 powder milk
¼ cup vegetable shortening, melted
4½ -5 ½ cups whole wheat flour

Pour warm water into a medium mixing bowl. Stir in honey and sprinkle yeast over surface. Set aside 5 to 10 minutes until foamy. Add salt, powdered milk, melted shortening, and 3 cups of whole wheat flour. Stir well, then beat until smooth. Add in cooked wheat and remaining flour and stir to make a stiff dough. Turn out onto a floured surface, cover and let rest for 5 minutes. Knead dough 10 minutes or until smooth and elastic. You may need to add surface flour to prevent sticking. Place dough in well-greased bowl and turn dough to grease all sides. Cover and let rise until doubled in size. Punch down and divide dough in half, roll out on floured surface into a 7" by 14" inch rectangle. Beginning at short side, roll tightly like a jellyroll. Pinch edge and ends to seal. Placed dough in 2 greased 9" by 5" bread pans seam side up. Turn dough placing the seamed side down, cover and set in warm place to rise above top of pan.

Preheat oven to 375 degrees. Bake about 25 minutes or until browned. Turn out of pans. Bread should sound hollow when tapped on bottom. Cool on a rack.

The kernels of wheat gives this bread a nutty flavor and texture. Very good.

Makes 2 loaves

A Favorite !

Wheat Quick Mix

8 C whole-wheat flour
½ cup + 2 tsp. baking soda
4 tsp. salt
2 cups vegetable shortening
¼ cup sugar

Sift all dry ingredients together twice. Cut in the vegetable shortening. Store in covered container in refrigerator. Will store for up to 2 months. This wheat quick mix can be used in most recipes calling for bisquick.

Wheat Quick Mix Muffins

2 cups wheat quick mix
2 Tbsp. brown sugar
1 egg
¾ cup milk
2 tbsp. vegetable oil

Mix all ingredients together well. Fill 12 greased muffins cups 2/3 full. Bake at 450 degrees for 15 minutes.

WHEAT

Wheat Quick Mix Biscuits

2 ¼ cups wheat quick mix
2/3 cup milk

Preheat oven to 450 degrees.

Blend wheat quick mix and milk together until soft dough is formed.

Dropped biscuits: Drop by tablespoonful onto an ungreased baking sheet. Bake for 8 to 10 minutes or until golden brown.

Rolled biscuits: Turn dough onto floured surface and knead gently 10 to 15 times. Roll out dough to ½ inch thickness. Cut with floured cookie cutter or the rim of a glass. Place on ungreased baking sheet and bake for 8 to 10 minutes or until golden brown.

Herbed Biscuits: Follow directions for dropped biscuits, adding ½ tsp. sage and ¼ thyme. These biscuit are wonderful served with poultry.

Garlicky Cheese Biscuits: Decrease wheat quick mix to 2 cups and add ¾ cup grated cheddar cheese to batter. Drop by spoonfuls onto an ungreased baking sheet. Bake for 10 minutes. Melt 2 ½ Tbsp. butter add ¼ tsp. garlic powder and brush over hot biscuits. Delicious!

Whole Wheat Bagels

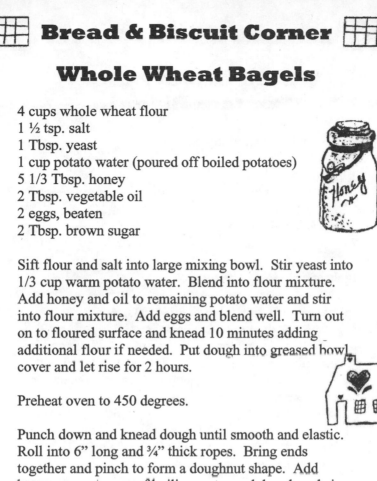

4 cups whole wheat flour
1 ½ tsp. salt
1 Tbsp. yeast
1 cup potato water (poured off boiled potatoes)
5 1/3 Tbsp. honey
2 Tbsp. vegetable oil
2 eggs, beaten
2 Tbsp. brown sugar

Sift flour and salt into large mixing bowl. Stir yeast into 1/3 cup warm potato water. Blend into flour mixture. Add honey and oil to remaining potato water and stir into flour mixture. Add eggs and blend well. Turn out on to floured surface and knead 10 minutes adding additional flour if needed. Put dough into greased bowl, cover and let rise for 2 hours.

Preheat oven to 450 degrees.

Punch down and knead dough until smooth and elastic. Roll into 6" long and ¾" thick ropes. Bring ends together and pinch to form a doughnut shape. Add brown sugar to pan of boiling water and drop bagels in one at a time. When they come to the top, turn over and boil for 1 more minute. Drain on a paper towel and place on an ungreased cookie sheet. Bake for 10 to 15 minutes or until golden brown

Cinnamon Bagels: Sift 2 Tbsp. cinnamon with flour mixture and add 1-cup raisins with eggs.

WHEAT

Whole Wheat Baking Powder Biscuits

1 cup whole-wheat pastry flour
4 tsp. baking powder
1 Tbsp. sugar
½ tsp. cream of tartar
½ tsp. salt
½ cup vegetable shortening
2/3 cup milk

Preheat oven to 450 degrees

In a large bowl, mix all dry ingredients. Cut in vegetable shortening with a pastry cutter or two knives, until mixture resembles course crumbs. Add milk and stir just until the dough all clings together in a ball. Drop by tablespoonful onto ungreased cookie sheet for dropped biscuits. For rolled biscuit, knead dough on lightly floured surface 10 to 12 times and roll out to ½ in thickness. Cut out with a floured biscuit cutter or rim of a glass. Bake on an ungreased baking sheet for 10 to 12 or until lightly browned.

Makes 1 dozen biscuits

From a friend:

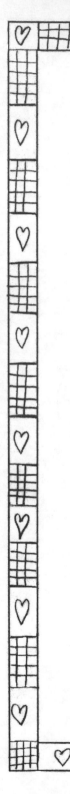

Whole Wheat Bread Made Easy

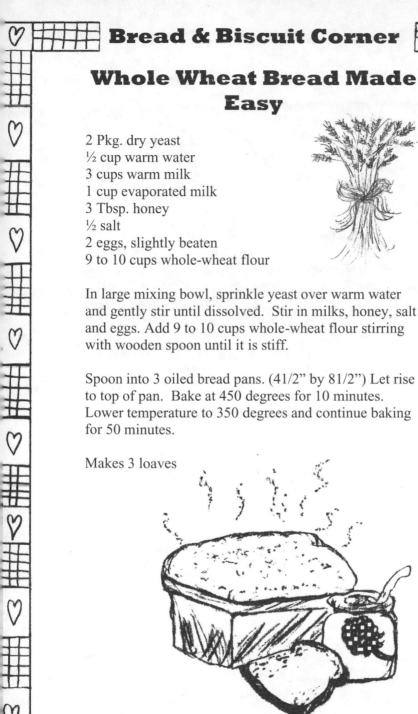

2 Pkg. dry yeast
½ cup warm water
3 cups warm milk
1 cup evaporated milk
3 Tbsp. honey
½ salt
2 eggs, slightly beaten
9 to 10 cups whole-wheat flour

In large mixing bowl, sprinkle yeast over warm water and gently stir until dissolved. Stir in milks, honey, salt and eggs. Add 9 to 10 cups whole-wheat flour stirring with wooden spoon until it is stiff.

Spoon into 3 oiled bread pans. (41/2" by 81/2") Let rise to top of pan. Bake at 450 degrees for 10 minutes. Lower temperature to 350 degrees and continue baking for 50 minutes.

Makes 3 loaves

Whole Wheat Bread

1¾ cups milk, scalded
2 tsp. salt
1/3 cup olive oil
1/3 honey
½ cup water
2 eggs
2 pkg. yeast
6 cups whole wheat flour

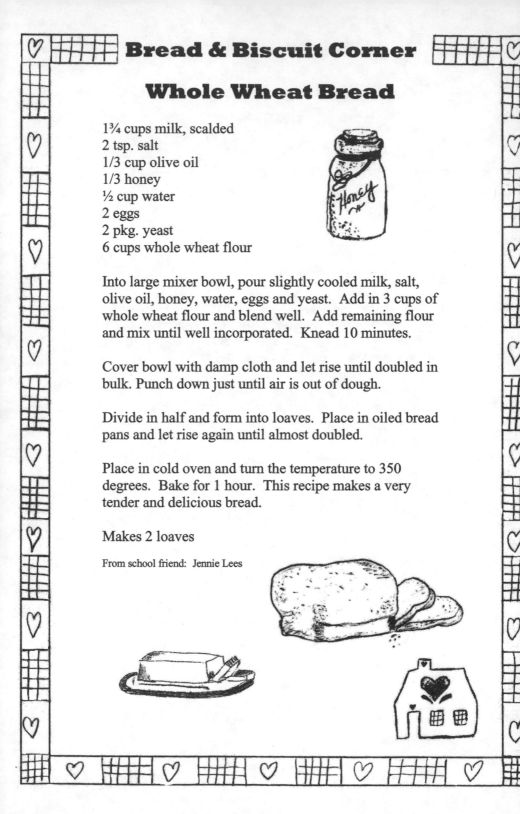

Into large mixer bowl, pour slightly cooled milk, salt, olive oil, honey, water, eggs and yeast. Add in 3 cups of whole wheat flour and blend well. Add remaining flour and mix until well incorporated. Knead 10 minutes.

Cover bowl with damp cloth and let rise until doubled in bulk. Punch down just until air is out of dough.

Divide in half and form into loaves. Place in oiled bread pans and let rise again until almost doubled.

Place in cold oven and turn the temperature to 350 degrees. Bake for 1 hour. This recipe makes a very tender and delicious bread.

Makes 2 loaves

From school friend: Jennie Lees

Whole Wheat Cottage Cheese Rolls

3 ¾ to 4 cups whole wheat flour
2 pkgs. Dry yeast
½ tsp. baking soda
1 ½ cup cream style cottage cheese
2 tsp. salt
½ cup water
1/3 cup packed brown sugar
2 Tbsp. butter or margarine
2 eggs

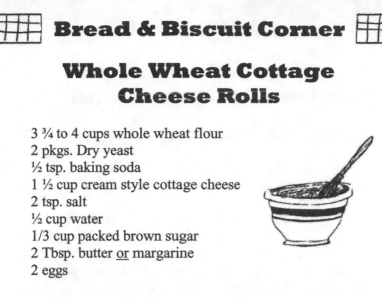

Thoroughly stir together 1 ½ cups flour, yeast and soda. Heat together cottage cheese, water, sugar, butter and salt just until warm (115-120 degrees) stirring constantly to melt butter. Add to dry mixture and add eggs. Beat at low speed on electric mixer for 30 seconds, scraping down bowl constantly. Beat on high speed for 3 minutes. By hand, stir enough remaining flour to make moderately stiff dough. Turn out on floured surface and knead until smooth. About 10 minutes. Place in greased bowl, turning once. Cover; let rise until nearly double. Punch down and shape into 24 rolls. Place into greased muffin pans. Let rise until doubled. Bake at 375 degrees for 12 to 15 minutes.

Makes 24 rolls

WHEAT

Whole Wheat Flour Tortillas/Pita Bread

5 cups whole wheat flour
1 tsp. salt
½ cup vegetable shortening
1 ½ to 2 cups hot water

In large bowl, combine flour and salt. Cut in vegetable shortening with a pastry cutter or two knifes. Place dough on floured surface and knead until it is pliable. Break off golf ball size pieces and roll each out to a 6" to 8" tortilla. They should be about 1/8 inch thick.

Cook on high in a large cast iron skillet or on a grill. As you cook the tortillas, bubbles will form. Cook until the bubbles are browned, turn and brown the other side, pushing down any large bubbles that form.

Pita bread: Follow the recipe above except you roll the dough ¼ inch thick and don't push down the bubbles.

A Favorite !

Bread & Biscuit Corner

Whole Wheat Onion Buns

3 Tbsp. butter <u>or</u> margarine
10 cups all-purpose flour
3 cups whole wheat flour
2 cups hot tap water
2 pkgs. Yeast
1 cup finely chopped onions
3 Tbsp. sugar
1½ tsp. salt

Sauté onions in butter until golden brown and set aside. In large mixer bowl, combine 1 cup all-purpose flour, 1 cup whole wheat flour, sugar, salt and yeast. Add hot water and all but 2 Tbsp. of onions and blend on low speed for 2 minutes. Add 1 cup whole wheat flour and beat on high speed for 2 minutes. Stir in remaining whole wheat flour and enough all-purpose flour (about 9 cups) to make a soft dough. Turn out on floured surface and knead until smooth and elastic. Place into a greased bowl, turn over to grease top and bottom of dough, cover and let rise in warm place until doubled in size. (About 1 hour). Punch down dough and divide into 20 equal parts. Roll each into a ball and place on a greased cookie sheet about 4½ inches apart. With buttered fingers press each into a 4-inch circle. Spread ¼ tsp. of reserved onion mixture onto each roll. Cover and let rise 45 minutes. Bake for 20 to 25 minutes at 375 degrees.

Yields: 20 large rolls, great for hamburgers.

From a friend:

Whole Wheat Rolls

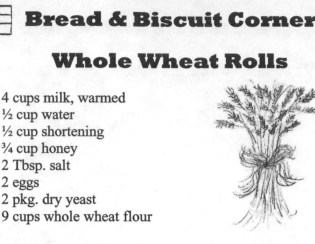

4 cups milk, warmed
½ cup water
½ cup shortening
¾ cup honey
2 Tbsp. salt
2 eggs
2 pkg. dry yeast
9 cups whole wheat flour

In a large mixing bowl, blend together the first six ingredients. Add 5 cups of whole wheat flour and blend with dough hook or wooden spoon until well blended. Add yeast and blend again. Add remaining 4 cups of flour and knead for 10 minutes with dough hook or turn out on floured surface and knead by hand for 15 minutes.

Place dough in large, lightly greased bowl and cover. Let rise until dough has doubled in size.

Roll out dough on floured surface to ½ inch thickness. Cut out with roll cutter or large drinking glass dipped in flour. Allow to rise until doubled and bake in 350-degree oven for 20 minutes.

From a friend:

Butters and Spreads

Honey Butter

½ cup butter
½ cup honey

Beat together until fluffy. Store in a covered container in refrigerator. The butter may softened in the microwave on high for 10 seconds at a time until desired consistency.

Cinnamon Butter

½ cup butter
½ cup brown sugar, packed
½ to 1 tsp. cinnamon

Beat all ingredients together until well blended. Store in refrigerator. This butter is especially good on hot bread just out of the oven.

Strawberry Butter

½ cup butter
½ cup strawberries, fresh or frozen
½ cup confectioner's sugar

Beat all ingredients together until well blended. Store in refrigerator. This flavored butter is fantastic on hot waffles.

Butters and Spreads

Orange-Honey Butter

½ cup butter
2 Tbsp. honey
1 tsp. grated orange peel
½ tsp. cinnamon

Beat all ingredients together until well blended. Store in refrigerator. Try this delightful butter on zucchini or nut bread.

Curry Butter

1 cup butter
2 tsp. curry powder

Blend together until light and fluffy. Great spread over hot corn on the cob!

Butters and Spreads

Herbed Butter

1 cup butter, room temperature
1 tsp. dried thyme, crushed
1 tsp. dried marjoram, crushed

Blend together all ingredients until well combined. Store in refrigerator.
Bring to room temperature before serving.

Basil-Tarragon Butter

1 cup butter
2 tsp. minced parsley
2 tsp. sweet basil, crushed
2 tsp. tarragon, crushed

Blend together all ingredients until well combined.
Fantastic served on baked potatoes.

Parmesan-Garlic Butter

1 cup butter
2/3 cup grated Parmesan cheese
½ tsp. garlic salt
2 Tbsp. snipped parsley <u>or</u> 2 tsp. dried parsley flakes

Beat butter, cheese and garlic salt until well blended.
Stir in parsley flakes. Cover and chill. Bring to room temperature before serving. This is excellent spread on French bread slices and put under the broiler until bubbly and browned.

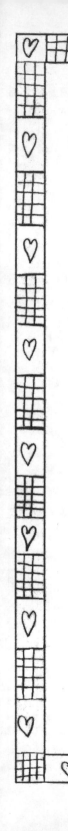

Bread & Biscuit Corner

Helpful Hints on Forming Bread Loaves:

1. Always make sure to preheat your oven before baking your bread.

2. Divide kneaded dough into number of loaves to be made. Cover with damp cloth and let rest.

3. You may shape loaf by patting or rolling. To pat dough, gently pull dough into a loaf shape, tucking under the edges. To shape dough by rolling, roll into a 12"x 8" rectangle on a lightly floured surface. Roll up tightly, starting at a narrow edge. Seal with fingertips as you roll.

4. Place each loaf, seam side down, into a greased bread pan.

5. For a soft and shiny crust, brush loaves with butter after baking. For a glossy, crispy crust, brush with milk, water or beaten egg before baking.

6. Test for doneness by tapping the top of the loaf with your finger, a hollow sound means bread is properly baked.

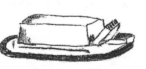

Bread Machine
Corner

Anise-Oat Wheat Bread

¾ cups regular rolled oats
1 cup milk
¼ cup water
2 Tbsp. butter
2 cups bread flour
1 cup whole wheat flour
1 tsp. salt
3 Tbsp. sugar
¾ tsp. anise seed
1½ tsp. active dry yeast

Pre heat oven to 350 degrees.

Spread oats in a shallow baking pan. Place oats in oven and cook for 15 minutes or until oats are lightly browned, stirring occasionally. Pour cooled oats into a blender or food processor and blend until finely ground. Add all of the ingredients to your machine, following manufacturer's directions. Select the whole grain cycle if you have it, if not; select the basic white bread cycle.

This bread is especially good toasted with honey.

Apple Bread

¾ cup apple juice
1/3 cup applesauce
1 Tbsp. butter
1 Tbsp. honey
1 cup whole wheat flour
2 cups bread flour
¾ salt
1 ½ tsp. cinnamon
½ tsp. nutmeg
1 tsp. dry active yeast

Add all of the ingredients to your machine, following the manufacturer's directions. Select the whole grain cycle if available, if not; select the basic white bread cycle.

Try this bread toasted with honey butter or use when making French toast. **YUMMY!**

Bread Machine Corner

Curried Wheat Bread

¾ cup milk
1 egg
3 Tbsp. water
1 Tbsp. butter
¾ cup whole wheat flour
2 ½ cup bread flour
1 Tbsp. sugar
1 tsp. curry powder
¾ tsp. salt
1¼ tsp. active yeast
¼ cup chopped peanuts

Add all of the ingredients into your machine, following the manufacturer's directions. Select the whole grain cycle if you have one, if not; select the white bread cycle.

From a dear friend.

Bread Machine Corner

Granola Cranapple Bread

1 ¼ cups buttermilk
2 Tbsp. honey
1 Tbsp. butter
¾ tsp. salt
1 ½ cup whole-wheat flour
1½ cups bread flour
1 Tbsp. gluten flour
1 tsp. active dry yeast
¾ cup apple granola (See breakfast section)
½ dried cranberries.

Add all of the ingredients to your machine, following the manufacturer's directions. Select the basic white bread recipe.

This bread makes the most wonderful toast. Great way to have a quick breakfast on the go.

40

Honey Anise Bread

1 cup milk
2 Tbsp. honey
1 Tbsp. water
1 Tbsp. butter
1½ cups whole wheat flour
1½ cups bread flour
2 tsp. gluten flour
1 Tbsp. anise seed, crushed
¾ tsp. salt
1 tsp. active dry yeast

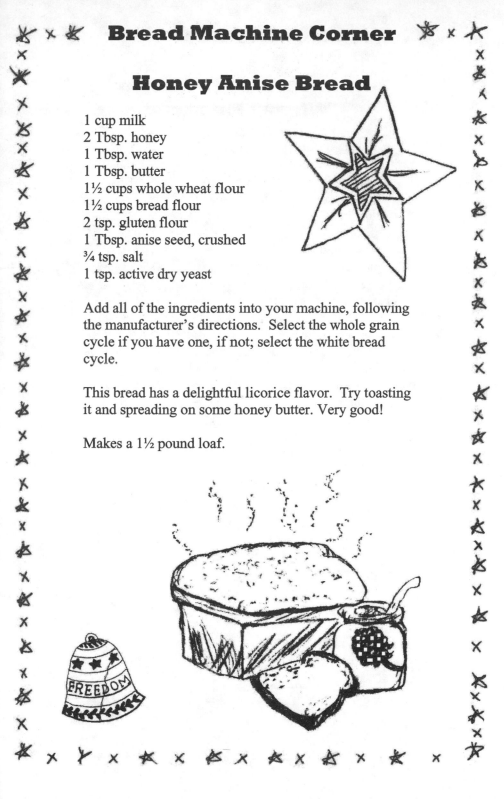

Add all of the ingredients into your machine, following the manufacturer's directions. Select the whole grain cycle if you have one, if not; select the white bread cycle.

This bread has a delightful licorice flavor. Try toasting it and spreading on some honey butter. Very good!

Makes a 1½ pound loaf.

Bread Machine Corner

Louisiana-Style Cajun Wheat Bread

½ cup diced green pepper
½ diced brown or purple onion
2 Tbsp. chili oil or vegetable oil
1 ½ to 2 tsp. Cajun spice seasoning
1 1/3 cups milk
3 Tbsp. honey
1 1/3 cups bread flour
2 2/3 cup whole-wheat flour
2 Tbsp. gluten flour
1 ¼ tsp. active dry yeast

Sauté the pepper and onion in the oil until vegetables are tender. Stir in the Cajun spices and cook for 30 seconds more. Remove from heat and set aside to cook slightly. Add all the ingredients to your machine following the manufacturer's directions, adding the peppers and onions with the milk.

The bread will spice up any meal.

This recipe makes a 2 pound loaf.

Mediterranean Fougasses Bread

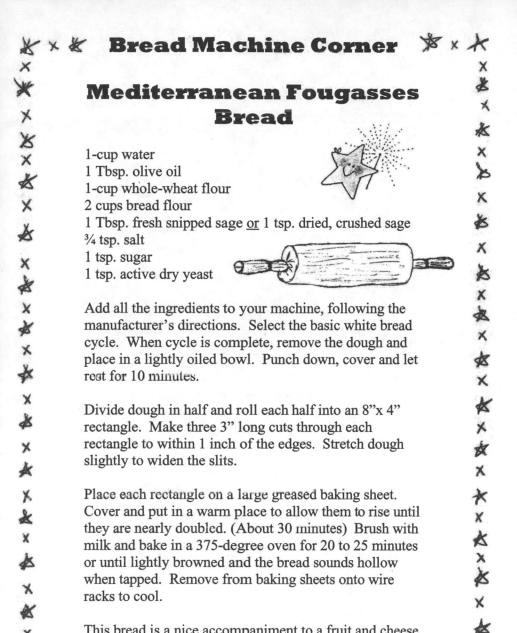

1-cup water
1 Tbsp. olive oil
1-cup whole-wheat flour
2 cups bread flour
1 Tbsp. fresh snipped sage <u>or</u> 1 tsp. dried, crushed sage
¾ tsp. salt
1 tsp. sugar
1 tsp. active dry yeast

Add all the ingredients to your machine, following the manufacturer's directions. Select the basic white bread cycle. When cycle is complete, remove the dough and place in a lightly oiled bowl. Punch down, cover and let rest for 10 minutes.

Divide dough in half and roll each half into an 8"x 4" rectangle. Make three 3" long cuts through each rectangle to within 1 inch of the edges. Stretch dough slightly to widen the slits.

Place each rectangle on a large greased baking sheet. Cover and put in a warm place to allow them to rise until they are nearly doubled. (About 30 minutes) Brush with milk and bake in a 375-degree oven for 20 to 25 minutes or until lightly browned and the bread sounds hollow when tapped. Remove from baking sheets onto wire racks to cool.

This bread is a nice accompaniment to a fruit and cheese platter.

Natural All Wheat Bread

This is Pam's favorite recipe for her Zojirushi bread machine.

1½ cups warm water
1 Tbsp. instant dry yeast
1/3 cup honey
3 cups whole wheat flour
2 Tbsp. vital gluten
1 tsp. dough enhancer
2 tsp. salt

Place yeast in the Zojirushi baking pan, add water. Mix with spatula until dissolved. Add honey, whole wheat flour, vital gluten, dough enhancer, and salt. Select basic white bread setting and press start.

This recipe make's a wonderful moist, light bread. It's a snap to make. I love it right out of the oven with lots of real butter. **YUMMY!**

Pineapple & Carrot Wheat bread

¾ cup buttermilk
1-8oz. can crushed pineapple (well drained)
½ cup shredded carrot
1 Tbsp. vegetable oil
1 cup bread flour
2 cups whole wheat flour
¾ tsp. salt
1 Tbsp. brown sugar
1 tsp. yeast

Add all of the ingredients to your machine, following the manufacturer's directions. Add the pineapple and carrots with the buttermilk. Select the whole grain cycle if your machine has one, if not; select the basic white bread cycle.

This delightful bread tastes wonderful with honey butter or makes a great peanut butter and jam sandwich.

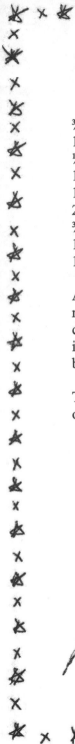

Roasted Garlic Wheat Bread

¾ cup water
1/3 cup sour cream
3 tsp. minced roasted garlic (bottled)
1 ½ cup whole wheat flour
1 ½ cup bread flour
2 tsp. gluten flour
¾ tsp. salt
1 tsp. sugar
1 tsp. active dry yeast

Add all of the ingredients to your machine, following the manufacturer's directions. Use the Whole grain cycle if available, if not select the white bread cycle.

Makes one 1½ pound loaf.

Rosemary Cracked Wheat Bread

1/3 cup cracked wheat
1 cup boiling water
1-cup milk
2 Tbsp. vegetable oil
2 cups whole wheat flour
1 cup bread flour
1 Tbsp. gluten flour
1 ¼ active dry yeast
1 Tbsp. brown sugar
¾ tsp. salt
1 ½ tsp. snipped fresh or ½ tsp. crushed dried rosemary
1 egg, beaten
1 Tbsp. water
1 Tbsp. fresh rosemary leaves

Stir cracked wheat into 1 cup boiling water; remove from heat and let stand for 3 minutes. Drain well and blend in milk. Add cracked wheat mixture and next 8 ingredients to your machine, following the manufacturer's directions. Select dough cycle. When the cycle is complete, remove dough from the machine. Punch down the dough, cover and let rest for 10 minutes. Place your dough on a lightly floured surface and shape into a ball. Place on greased baking sheet and flatten slightly to a 6-inch round loaf. Cover dough and allow to rise in a warm place until nearly doubled. (About 45 to 55 minutes) Combine beaten egg with water and brush over bread. Sprinkle with fresh rosemary leaves.

Bake in a 350-degree oven for 35 to 40 minutes or until bread sounds hollow when lightly tapped. If bread is overbrowning, loosely cover with foil for last 10 to 15 minutes of baking. Cool on a wire rack.

Sourdough Baked Pretzel

1 ¼ cups sourdough starter
1 ½ cups bread flour
1 1/3 cups whole wheat flour
1 Tbsp. vital wheat gluten
2 Tbsp. milk
¾ tsp. salt
1 Tbsp. sugar
1 tsp. active dry yeast
1 beaten egg
1 Tbsp. water

1 egg
1 Tbsp. water
kosher salt

Preheat oven to 350 degrees.

Add first 8 ingredients to the machine according the manufacturer's directions. Select dough cycle. When cycle has been completed, remove the dough from the machine and place into a large lightly greased bowl. Punch down and let rest for 10 minutes.

On a lightly floured surface, roll dough into a 14"x8" rectangle. Cut into 14"x ½ " strips. Gently pull each strip into a 16- inch rope. Shape the ropes into pretzels or leave as pretzel rods. Place on greased baking sheets. Do not let them rise. Beat egg and water together and brush over pretzels. Sprinkle with kosher salt and bake for 18 to 20 minutes or until golden brown.

Bake 1 sheet of pretzels at a time. Keep remaining sheets in the refrigerator to prevent pretzels from rising.

Makes 16 pretzels or rods.

Bread Machine Corner

Sourdough Wheat Bread

1 ¼ cup sourdough starter
½ milk or you may use water if desired
1 Tbsp. vegetable oil
¼ cup toasted wheat germ
2 cups whole wheat flour
1 cup bread flour
2 Tbsp. gluten flour
1 ½ Tbsp. brown sugar
¾ tsp. salt
1 tsp. active dry yeast

Add ingredients to your machine, following the manufacturer's directions. Use the whole grain cycle if available on your machine. If not, select the white bread cycle. This recipe makes a hearty 1 ½ pound loaf. The addition of the wheat germ adds a wonderful texture to the bread.

This bread makes super sourdough French toast.

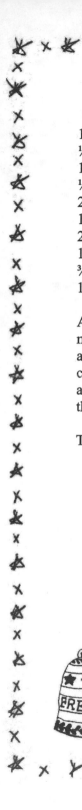

49

Bread Machine Corner

Tomato & Herb Bread

¾ cup water
¼ cup snipped dried tomatoes (not oil-packed)
½ tomato sauce
4 tsp. butter
1 1/3 cups whole wheat flour
2 2/3 cups bread flour
1 Tbsp. snipped fresh oregano or 1½ tsp. dried, crushed oregano
1 Tbsp. brown sugar
¾ tsp. salt
1 ¼ tsp. yeast

Add all of the ingredients to your machine, following the manufacturer's directions, adding the tomatoes with the water. Use the whole grain cycle if available, if not select the basic white bread cycle.

Great served with your favorite soup and salad.

Bread Machine Corner

Whole Wheat Bread

1-cup milk
3 Tbsp. water
4 tsp. honey
1 Tbsp. butter
1 ½ cup bread flour
1 ½ cup whole-wheat flour
¾ tsp. salt
1 tsp. active dry yeast

Add all of the ingredients into your machine, following the manufacturer's directions. Use the whole grain cycle if you have it, if not; select the basic white bread cycle.

This recipe makes a 1½ pound loaf.

Whole Wheat Cornmeal Bread

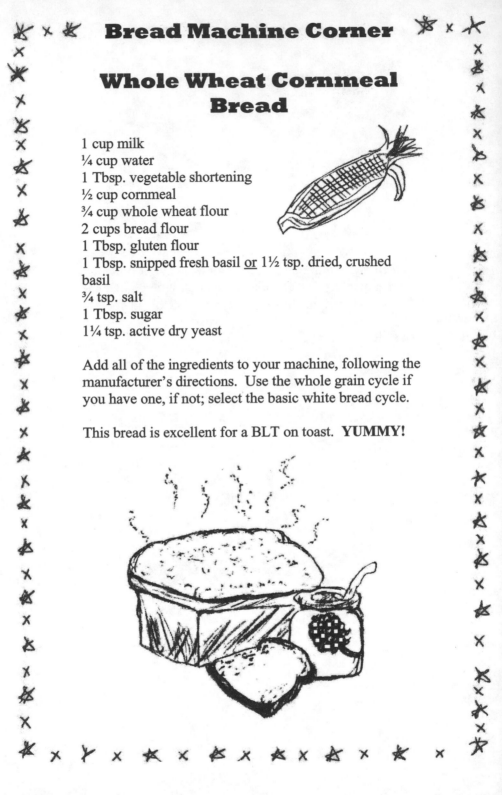

1 cup milk
¼ cup water
1 Tbsp. vegetable shortening
½ cup cornmeal
¾ cup whole wheat flour
2 cups bread flour
1 Tbsp. gluten flour
1 Tbsp. snipped fresh basil <u>or</u> 1½ tsp. dried, crushed basil
¾ tsp. salt
1 Tbsp. sugar
1¼ tsp. active dry yeast

Add all of the ingredients to your machine, following the manufacturer's directions. Use the whole grain cycle if you have one, if not; select the basic white bread cycle.

This bread is excellent for a BLT on toast. **YUMMY!**

Whole Wheat Soup Bowls

1 cup milk
2 eggs
¼ cup butter
4 cups whole wheat pastry flour
4 tsp. sugar
1 tsp. salt
1 ¼ tsp. active dry yeast
¾ cup shredded cheese, Colby jack, cheddar, Swiss or Monterey jack.

Preheat oven to 350 degrees.

Add first 7 ingredients to your machine, following the manufacturer's directions. Select the basic white bread cycle on your machine. When the cycle is complete, remove the dough from your machine. Punch down. Cover and let rest for 10 minutes.

Generously grease the outside of 6 each 10 oz. bowls. Place them upside down on greased cookie sheets, allowing 3 inches between bowls. Divide your dough into 6 portions. On a lightly floured surface, roll out each portion into a 12"x6"rectangle. Sprinkle about 2 Tbsp. cheese onto half of each rectangle to within ½ inch of the edges. Moisten edges; fold each rectangle in half to form a 6" square. Seal edges.

Drape the dough squares over the bowls, pressing lightly. Immediately place in oven and bake for 20 to 25 minutes or until lightly browned.

These bowls are wonderful for soups, stews, beans or chili.

For a great dessert bowl: omit the cheese and sprinkle with cinnamon and sugar. Fill with ice cream, fruit or rice pudding. **YUMMY!**

Wild Rice Bread

¾ cup cooked wild rice, drained well and cooled completely
1 cup water
4 tsp. butter
1 cup whole wheat flour
2 cups bread flour
1¼ tsp. instant chicken bouillon granules
1 Tbsp. sugar
¾ tsp. salt
½ tsp. dried thyme, crushed
1 tsp. active yeast

Add all of the ingredients to your machine, following the manufacturer's directions. Select the whole grain cycle if you have one, if not; select the white bread cycle.

The wild rice in this recipe gives the bread a nutty and chewy texture. Try using your favorite cheese and a slice of ripe tomato to create a tasty grilled cheese sandwich.

Zucchini Wheat Bread

1 cup milk
1 ½ cups grated zucchini
2 Tbsp. vegetable shortening
2 2/3 cups whole wheat flour
1 1/3 cups bread flour
2 tbsp. gluten flour
1 ½ Tbsp. brown sugar
2 tsp. finely grated lemon peel
1 tsp. salt
2 tsp. yeast

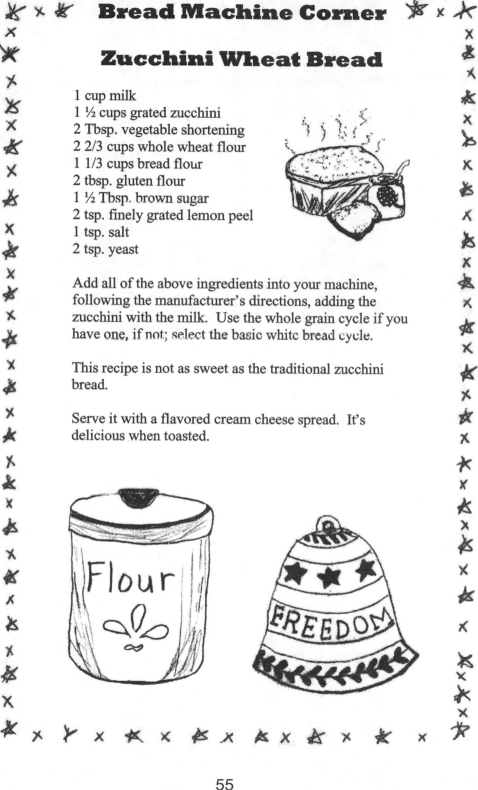

Add all of the above ingredients into your machine, following the manufacturer's directions, adding the zucchini with the milk. Use the whole grain cycle if you have one, if not; select the basic white bread cycle.

This recipe is not as sweet as the traditional zucchini bread.

Serve it with a flavored cream cheese spread. It's delicious when toasted.

Breakfast Corner

Banana Stuffed French Toast

4 slices sourdough bread, cut 1½" thick
2 bananas cut into ½ inch slices
2 eggs
¾ cup milk
1 tsp. vanilla
Butter <u>or</u> vegetable oil for frying
1/3 cup sugar and 1 tsp. cinnamon, combined
Maple syrup

Cut a pocket in top of each bread slice. Fill pockets with banana slices. Beat eggs, milk and vanilla together in a shallow dish. Dip stuffed bread into egg mixture. Leave in mixture a few seconds to allow the milk to soak into bread, turning once or twice. Heat butter in frying pan. Cook bread slices until golden brown on both sides. Drain on a paper towel and sprinkle with sugar and cinnamon mixture. Serve with butter and warmed maple syrup.

I like to sprinkle chopped pecans on top of the warmed maple syrup for a little added flavor and crunch

Makes 2 to 4 servings

From a dear friend: Sandy Phelps

Yummy

Breakfast Corner

Buttermilk Pancakes

Combine ingredients in order listed:

2 cups flour (1½ cup all-purpose & ½ cup whole wheat)
¼ tsp. salt
1 tsp. baking powder
1½ tsp. baking powder
2 eggs
2 1/3 cup buttermilk

Mix together all ingredients until you have a batter. Pour onto a hot griddle. Serve warm.

Powerhouse Pancakes

1 cup whole-wheat flour
1½ tsp. baking powder
1-1/3 cup bran
½ cup soy flakes
2 Tbsp. honey
1 Tbsp. vegetable oil
1¾ cup – 2 cups buttermilk
4 egg whites, beaten

Mix dry ingredients together. Add remaining ingredients to beaten eggs. Combine the two mixtures in a medium bowl. Adjust buttermilk to thickness of batter desired. Cook on a slightly oiled griddle. Make 3 servings.

Cream Cheese French Toast

1 8 oz. pkg. cream cheese, softened
1 tsp. vanilla
½ cup chopped walnuts or pecans
1 long loaf sourdough bread, sliced into 12 – 1½" slices
4 eggs
1 cup whipping cream
½ tsp. vanilla
¼ tsp. nutmeg
Butter <u>or</u> vegetable oil for frying
1 12 oz. jar apricot jam
½ cup orange juice

Beat together cream cheese and 2 tsp. vanilla until fluffy. Stir in chopped nuts. Place 2 tsp. of cream cheese mixture into each slice of bread. Beat together eggs, cream, vanilla and nutmeg in a shallow dish. Dip bread slices into egg mixture, turning bread over twice to absorb the liquid. Heat butter in pan and cook bread on both sides until golden brown. Keep warm on baking sheet in oven. In a small bowl, combine apricot jam and orange juice. Heat in microwave. Drizzle hot jam mixture over French toast and dust with powdered sugar.

You may use orange marmalade in place of apricot jam if desired.

This is a wonderful recipe for a brunch. French toast can be made a head of time and kept warm in a 250-degree oven so that everyone can be served together.

Makes 6 servings, 2 slices each.

From a dear friend: Jen Cragun

Breakfast Corner

Cream of Wheat

Stir together:
1-cup coarse wheat flour (a farina texture)
1-cup cool water

In a saucepan bring to a boil:
1-cup water

Gradually add the first mixture stirring continuously on a low boil until think, about 1 minute. Add salt and honey to taste. Serve warm with milk or juice.

For leftovers, stir in brown pork sausage <u>or</u> ground beef and put in rectangular dish and chill. Then slice into serving pieces approximately ½" thick and sauté in butter. Serve with hot syrup.

Syrup from Honey

Honey
Water

Combine equal parts honey and water. Mix together and bring to a boil. Simmer for 5 minutes.

Breakfast Corner

Granola Cereal

6 cups oats
6 cups rolled wheat
2 cups coconut (optional)
1 cup raisins or dates, dried apples or apricots
2 cups honey or raw or dark brown sugar
3 tsp. salt
3 tsp. vanilla
1½ cup vegetable oil
1½ cup hot water
Wheat germ (optional)

If honey is used, dissolve it in the hot water. Combine ingredients. Mix well and spread on two large cookie sheets. Bake at 250 degrees for 2 hours stirring often.

Serve with cold milk

Nutritional Dry Cereal Mix

4 cups oatmeal
1 Tbsp. sunflower seeds
1 cup whole-wheat flour
2½ cups wheat germ
1 cup coconut
2 tsp. cinnamon

2 Tbsp. sesame seeds
½ cup almonds
1 cup corn meal
1 tsp. vanilla
½ cup honey
1/3 cup vegetable oil

Combine dry ingredients and mix well. Add honey, vanilla, and oil. Mix thoroughly (with hands). Spread evenly on 2 large ungreased pans and bake 30 minutes at 300 degrees. Stir every 10 minutes so it toasts evenly. You can add dates, raisins, apples, raspberries or any other dried fruits to this mix.

Store in an airtight container.

Breakfast Corner

GREAT Utah Farm Hotcakes

1 cup whole-wheat flour
½ tsp. baking soda
¼ tsp. salt
1 ½ tsp. baking powder
1 Tbsp. brown sugar
1 cup buttermilk
1 Tbsp. oil
2 eggs

Mix first five ingredients together and then add the buttermilk, eggs and oil. Thin mixture with milk <u>or</u> water.

Whole Wheat Pancakes

Soak ¾ cup wheat and put in refrigerator overnight. In the morning, drain and blend softened wheat in a blender with 1 cup milk for 4 minutes. Blend in 1 Tbsp. honey. Add 3 egg yolks and blend 2 minutes. Add 3 egg whites and blend another 2 minutes. This makes thin pancakes that are delicious !

Cook on hot griddle….

From a friend: Lisa Pantone

Breakfast Corner

Homemade Grape Nuts

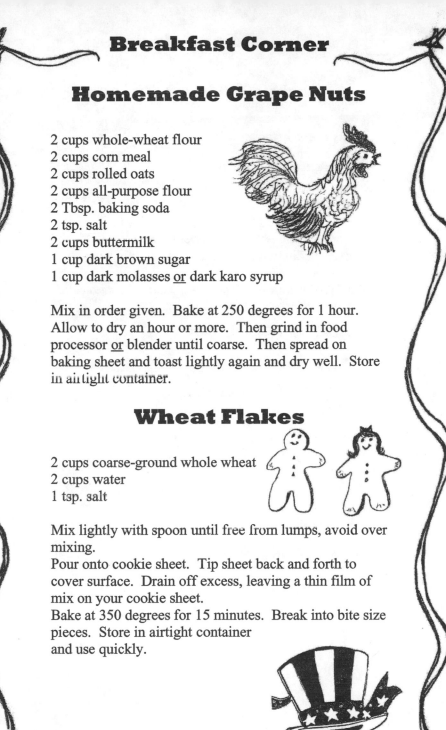

2 cups whole-wheat flour
2 cups corn meal
2 cups rolled oats
2 cups all-purpose flour
2 Tbsp. baking soda
2 tsp. salt
2 cups buttermilk
1 cup dark brown sugar
1 cup dark molasses <u>or</u> dark karo syrup

Mix in order given. Bake at 250 degrees for 1 hour.
Allow to dry an hour or more. Then grind in food
processor <u>or</u> blender until coarse. Then spread on
baking sheet and toast lightly again and dry well. Store
in airtight container.

Wheat Flakes

2 cups coarse-ground whole wheat
2 cups water
1 tsp. salt

Mix lightly with spoon until free from lumps, avoid over
mixing.
Pour onto cookie sheet. Tip sheet back and forth to
cover surface. Drain off excess, leaving a thin film of
mix on your cookie sheet.
Bake at 350 degrees for 15 minutes. Break into bite size
pieces. Store in airtight container
and use quickly.

India Wheat Cakes

2 cups cooked cracked wheat
½ cup chopped onions
½ cup fresh mint <u>or</u> parsley
2 Tbsp. dry milk
2 eggs, beaten

Mix and season with salt/pepper to taste, fry patties in oil over medium heat in skillet until lightly browned.

This is great for breakfast, use instead of potato cakes with your eggs and bacon/sausage.

From a friend: Jeri Brown

Wheat Berries & Raisin Sauce

Add 2 cups steamed wheat to sauce (below). Heat and serve. Good as cereal, snack or pudding.

2 cups water
1 cup raisins
1 tsp. vinegar (cider)
3 Tbsp. honey
2 Tbsp. cornstarch

Cook raisins and water for 10 minutes. Make a paste with the vinegar, honey and cornstarch. Add to raisin mixture. Stir until thick and smooth.

From a friend: Jeri Brown

Breakfast Corner

Nutty Granola

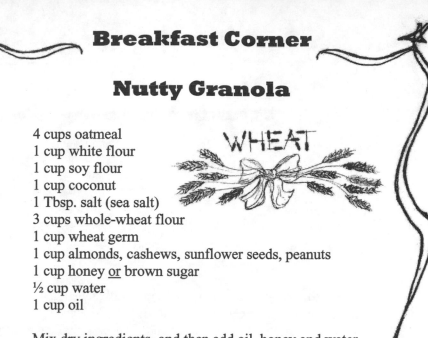

4 cups oatmeal
1 cup white flour
1 cup soy flour
1 cup coconut
1 Tbsp. salt (sea salt)
3 cups whole-wheat flour
1 cup wheat germ
1 cup almonds, cashews, sunflower seeds, peanuts
1 cup honey <u>or</u> brown sugar
½ cup water
1 cup oil

Mix dry ingredients, and then add oil, honey and water. Mix with hands. Mixture should be crumbly. Add more water for bigger crumbs. Put into 2 large flat pans and bake at 250-300 degrees for 1 hour. Turn mixture every 20 minutes

Keep in airtight container.

Overnight Cinnamon French Toast

3 eggs
½ cup milk
1/8 tsp. baking powder
¼ tsp. cinnamon
1 tsp. vanilla
6-1½" thick slices of sourdough bread
4 Tbsp. butter <u>or</u> margarine

In a medium bowl, beat together eggs, milk, sugar, baking powder, cinnamon and vanilla. Place bread slices on a rimmed baking sheet and pour egg mixture over top. Turn each slice of bread over to be sure all bread is coated with egg mixture. Cover baking sheet with plastic wrap and refrigerate overnight. To prepare French toast, melt butter in large frying pan and fry bread slices on both sides until golden brown. Serve with Cinnamon syrup.

Cinnamon Syrup

1 cup sugar   ½ cup light corn syrup
¼ cup water   1 tsp. cinnamon
½ cup whipping cream

In a small saucepan, stir together sugar, corn syrup, water and cinnamon. Stirring constantly, bring to boil and boil for 2 minutes over medium heat. Remove from heat and stir in cream. Cool. I prepare this the night before then warm slightly in the microwave.
This recipe is easily doubled. It takes about 10 minutes from refrigerator to the table. Perfect for those early school mornings or for a quick Sunday morning breakfast.

From a dear friend: Sandy Phelps

Pancake Toppers

Caramel Banana Topping

1 cup caramel topping
2 medium bananas
¼ cup pecans or walnuts (optional)

To make topping, heat caramel topping until warm.
Gently stir in bananas and pecans. Add to top of
pancakes while warm.

Maple Orange Syrup

1 cup maple-flavored syrup (any brand)
3 Tbsp. orange juice
3 Tbsp. butter or margarine

Heat all the ingredients in 1-qt. saucepan over medium
Heat, stirring occasionally until warm. Pour over
pancakes while warm.

Pear-Raspberry Topping

¼ cup sugar
½ cup water
1 Tbsp. finely chopped crystallized ginger (optional)
2 tsp. cornstarch
2 tsp. butter or margarine
1½ tsp. lemon juice
2 medium pear, peeled and sliced
½ cup raspberries

Heat all ingredients above except the pears and
raspberries in a saucepan over medium heat until
mixture boils. Boil 1 minute. Stir in pears, heat
through. Stir in raspberries. Top pancakes while warm.

Pancake Toppers

Honey Syrup

1 cup honey
1 cube butter <u>or</u> margarine
½ tsp. cinnamon

heat honey and butter in a saucepan over low heat until melted. Add cinnamon. Stir well. Add to top of pancakes while warm.

Apple Topping (GREAT for the German Pancakes or Crepes)

3 med-large apples (your preference on taste)
1 Tbsp. flour	¼ tsp. salt
¼ cup brown sugar	1/8 tsp. ginger
¼ cup white sugar	1½ tsp. lemon juice
¾ tsp. cinnamon	2 Tbsp. butter <u>or</u>
¼ tsp. nutmeg	margarine

Cook apples adding enough water not to burn. Cook until firm. Add the rest of ingredients with the exception of the flour. Add a small amount of cold water to the flour to make a paste and then add to the filling. Cook until thick. Cool and pour over pancakes, waffles or fill German pancakes or crepes.

You can also top with whipping cream. YUMMY!

Spiced Pancakes

2½ tsp. baking powder
½ cup white flour
½ cup whole-wheat flour
½ cup oat bran
½ cup wheat germ
½ tsp. ginger

1 tsp. cinnamon
1 cup milk
½ cup cottage cheese
¼ cup vegetable oil
¼ cup orange honey
1 egg or 4 Tbsp. egg substitute

Mix all dry ingredients together. Stir together milk, cheese, vegetable oil and honey. Add dry ingredients to the liquid. Beat all together until smooth. Drop by spoonfuls on hot, spray-greased skillet. Turn when bubbly.

See the pancake toppers pages in this corner for a variety of flavors to try on top of your pancakes....

Take Along Breakfast Treat

1 cup light brown sugar, packed to measure
½ cup butter or margarine, at room temperature
½ cup peanut butter
1 large egg
1 tsp. vanilla extract
1 cup old-fashioned oats
1 cup light or dark seedless raisins

¾ cup whole-wheat flour
½ cup nonfat dry milk
¼ cup wheat germ
¾ tsp. salt
¼ tsp. baking powder
¼ tsp. baking soda
3 Tbsp. milk
3 Tbsp. sesame seeds

In a large bowl, beat sugar, butter and peanut butter until smooth. Beat in egg and vanilla. When well blended, add remaining ingredients except the sesame seeds, mix well.

Divide dough into 9 equal parts, using about ¼ cup dough for each part. Put pieces of dough several inches apart on greased baking sheet; pat into circles about 4½" in diameter. Sprinkle with sesame seeds.

Heat oven to 375 degrees. Bake 10 to 12 minutes, until cookies are lightly browned around edges. Cool 5 minutes on baking sheet; remove to a wire rack and cool completely.

Makes 9 large treats

Breakfast Corner

Thermos Wheat Cereal

½ - 1 cup wheat kernels (berries)
1 quart boiling water   *Yummy*

Put wheat berries into a thermos and add boiling water to thermos. Screw on lid and let sit for 2 hours or the easiest is to let stand overnight. Strain. Serve with milk and honey or sugar.

A Favorite !

My kids love these wheat berries with concentrated apple juice poured over them. They are the best little treat for a quick breakfast.

Whole Wheat Cereal

1 cup whole-wheat kernels (berries)
2 cups water
¼ tsp. salt

Bring water to a boil and add wheat kernels and salt. Cook until kernels (berries) are tender, about 20 minutes. Serve with milk and sugar or honey. Also, as above you can pour concentrated apple juice over the berries instead of milk. It then does not need honey or sugar. This can also be cooked in a crock-pot overnight and is ready to serve when you wake up.

Cracked Bulgur

2 cups dried cracked bulgur
2 cups water

Boil for 5 minutes. Sweeten to taste and serve hot.

Breakfast Corner

Whole Wheat Blender Pancakes

Easy Easy Easy

Place in a blender at high speed for 2 – 3 minutes

1½ cups milk
1 cup whole-wheat berries (uncooked)
Add the following and blend 1 minute more.
1 egg
1 tsp. salt
1/3 cup cooking oil
2/3 tsp. baking powder
2 Tbsp. sugar or honey

Note: Some wheat blends up thicker than others. You will need to adjust the liquid if batter is too thick.

You can also use powdered milk and powdered eggs in this recipe.

Variations:
Buttermilk pancakes: Substitute 1 cup buttermilk for the regular milk.

Rolled whole-wheat pancakes: Substitute 2 cups rolled whole-wheat for the whole-wheat berries.

Rolled oats pancakes: Substitute 2 1/3 cups rolled oats for the whole-wheat berries.

Whole Wheat Buttermilk Hot Cakes

1½ cups whole-wheat flour
1 Tbsp. baking powder
¾ tsp. salt
3 Tbsp. brown sugar

2 egg yolks
1½ cups buttermilk
3 Tbsp. oil
2 egg whites, beaten

Combine in order given, folding in beaten egg whites last. Bake on lightly greased hot griddle. Sugar can be omitted.

From a friend: Sandy Phelps

More – Wheat Buttermilk Pancakes

3 cups whole-wheat flour
3 tsp. baking powder
1/3 cup oil
3 eggs, *reconstituted, or
3 fresh eggs
3 cups buttermilk or powdered milk

Mix all ingredients together with a wire whip. If dough is too thick, add ½ cup water.

Buttermilk makes a lighter pancake.
*Dehydrated eggs, to reconstitute, mix 1 Tbsp. water with 1 Tbsp whole egg powder. Beat in a blender to get rid of the lumps.

Whole Wheat Crepes

4 eggs
4 Tbsp. whole-wheat flour
a pinch of salt
2 cups milk

Beat eggs and salt together. Add flour and beat slightly. Gradually add milk. Melt a small amount of butter in a pan. Pour a thin layer of batter over the entire surface of pan. Cook over medium heat for a short period until bottom is slightly browned. Turn it over and cook lightly. Remove from the pan.

Top crepes with fresh fruit, pudding, jam, tuna, chicken, or cream cheese filling, adding a little powdered sugar sprinkled on top or even ice cream. Roll up and eat. Crepes may be served as a main dish or as a dessert.

German Pancakes
Similar to crepes

5 eggs
2½ cups milk
1 cup whole-wheat flour or 1 cup all-purpose flour or
half wheat and half white flour
pinch of salt

Blend all ingredients in a blender or beat well by hand. Pour small amounts into a greased frying Pan. Fry like a crepe.

These are great served with strawberries and whipping cream or sour cream on top.

Whole Wheat Waffles

4 eggs
1½ cup milk
4 Tbsp. oil
1 Tbsp. honey
Blend all the above ingredients in a blender. Then add:
2 cups wheat flour
2 tsp. baking powder
½ tsp. salt
Cook in a heated waffle iron.

From a friend: Lisa Pantone

Waffles

1. Beat 2 eggs
2. Add and beat until smooth:
    2 cups buttermilk <u>or</u> sour milk
    1 tsp. soda
    2 cups whole-wheat flour
    2 tsp. baking powder
    ½ tsp. salt
    6 Tbsp. shortening or bacon grease
3. This is a thin batter. Bake in a hot waffle iron.
4. Pour ½ cup batter into center of waffle iron. Bake about 5 minutes <u>or</u> until golden brown.

Regular milk may be used. Omit the soda and use 4 tsp. baking powder instead. Separate eggs. Beat egg whites until stiff and fold in last.

Makes 8 waffles.

From a friend:

Yummy Granola

4 cups oatmeal
½ cup chopped almonds
1 cup coconut
1 cup whole-wheat flour
1-10oz. jar wheat germ
1/3 cup brown sugar
1 tsp. vanilla
½ cup honey
1/3 cup vegetable oil
1 cup milk (you can use powdered milk)

Mix all the dry ingredients together and set aside. Blend liquid ingredients together. Pour over the dry ingredients and mix with your hands. Spread on flat cookie sheets and bake for 30 minutes at 300 degrees. Stir every 10 minutes or so.

Apple Granola

4 cups oats
3 cups chopped apples
¾ cup whole-wheat flour
½ cup chopped walnuts or pecans
¼ cup packed brown sugar
½ cup chopped dates or raisins

½ tsp. cinnamon
¼ tsp. salt
1 cup apple juice

¼ cup oil
1 tsp. vanilla

Combine oats, apples, flour, walnuts, brown sugar, cinnamon and salt; mix well. Heat apple juice; add oat mixture and let stand 15 minutes or until softened. Mash and blend well, beat in oil and vanilla. Add dates, place in a thin layer on greased baking sheets. Bake at 350 degrees for 10 min. Reduce heat to 250 degrees and bake one hour. Stir and bake 1½ to 2 hours longer or until mixture is dry, stirring every 30 minutes or so.

From a friend:

Crackers & Pastas Corner

Crackers & Pastas Corner

Easy Soft Pretzels

1 pkg. active yeast
11/3 cups warm water
1 Tbsp. sugar
½ tsp. salt
2 cups whole wheat flour
1½ -2 cups all-purpose flour
1 egg beaten with1 Tbsp. water
2 Tbsp. kosher salt or sesame seeds

Preheat oven to 425 degrees

In a large bowl, sprinkle yeast over warm water. Stir with rubber spatula until yeast is dissolved. Gently stir in sugar and salt until completely dissolved. Using a wooden spoon, gradually stir in 3½ cups flour until a stiff dough forms. Place dough on a floured surface and 5 to 7 minutes until smooth, you may need to add a ½ cup or more of flour at this time. Divide dough into 12 equal pieces and allow to rest for 5 to 10 minutes. Roll each piece into a 15" rope and twist into a pretzel shape. Place on greased cookie sheet and brush with beaten egg mixture. Sprinkle with salt or sesame seeds and bake until golden brown, about 25 minutes.

May be served warm or cold.

Crackers & Pastas Corner

Easy Whole Wheat Pizza Crust

2 cups whole wheat flour
1 Tbsp. active dry yeast
¾ tsp. salt
1 tsp. honey
1 Tbsp. olive oil

Combine flour, yeast and salt in large bowl. Add water, oil and honey; mix well. Cover with a damp cloth and place in a warm spot for 10 minutes to rise. Punch down and press into a greased 14 inch pizza pan or, for a thick crust, use a 10 inch pan. Spread your favorite sauce and toppings on crust and bake at 425 degrees for 15 to 20 minutes. Crust should be golden brown and cheese melted.

Family Size Pizza Crust Recipe

4 cups warm water
4 Tbsp. active yeast
4 Tbsp. sugar
½ cup olive oil
4 tsp. salt
10 cups whole wheat flour

Stir warm water, yeast, and sugar together in large bowl and let sit for 10 minutes. Stir in remaining ingredients and let sit for an additional 30 minutes. Divide dough into four equal parts and roll to 1/8 inch thick. Place in pizza pans, top with sauce, cheese and your favorite toppings. Bake at 375 degrees for 20 Minutes.

Feeds a crowd!

Crackers & Pastas Corner

Homemade Whole Wheat Noodles

1-cup whole-wheat flour
1 large egg, well beaten
2 Tbsp. milk
½ tsp. salt

Mix flour, egg, milk and salt to make a stiff ball of dough. On a lightly floured surface roll our your dough until it is very thin. It should be about 18" by 20". Let dry for 1½ hours. Using a pastry cutter or sharp knife, cut into ½ inch strips. Drop into boiling lightly salted water or your favorite soup and cook for 8 to 10 minutes.

Makes 3 cups

Crackers & Pastas Corner

Homemade Whole Wheat Pasta

1-cup whole-wheat flour
1 large egg, well beaten
2 Tbsp. milk
½ tsp. salt

Mix flour, egg, milk and salt to make a stiff ball of dough. On a lightly floured surface roll our your dough until it is very thin. It should be about 18" by 20". Let dry for 1½ hours. Using a pastry cutter or sharp knife, cut into ½ inch strips. Drop into boiling lightly salted water or your favorite soup and cook for 8 to 10 minutes.

Makes 3 cups

From a friend: Kristen Anderson

Crackers & Pastas Corner

Letter Shaped Pretzels

1 cup all-purpose flour
½ cup whole wheat flour
1½ tsp. baking powder
1 tsp. sugar
¼ tsp. salt
2/3 cup milk
2 Tbsp. softened butter <u>or</u> margarine
1 egg
Kosher salt. sesame, poppy or celery seeds, or any herb you like.

Preheat oven to 400 degrees

Combine flour, baking powder, sugar and salt in a large bowl and mix well. Add milk and softened butter and stir to form a soft dough. Knead dough on lightly floured surface about 40 times or until the dough is soft and smooth. Tear off small pieces of dough about the size of a walnut. Dust you hands with flour and roll each piece into a pencil thin rope about 5 inches long. Shape the dough into desired letters and place on a lightly greased baking sheet. Bake 10 minutes or until golden brown.

Crackers & Pastas Corner

Pam's Wheat Chips

1 cup whole wheat flour
2 cups cold water

Stir wheat flour and water together in a medium mixing bowl.

Season mixture with the following:

½ tsp. each, onion and garlic salt
1-tsp. salt or vegetable salt substitute.
3 to 4 Tbsp. Parmesan cheese
or 1 Tbsp. of your favorite dry seasoning like taco,
barbecue or French onion soup mix

Stir ingredients together. Pour mixture into a squirt
bottle and squirt desired size chips onto a cookie sheet
that has been sprayed with cooking spray. Sprinkle
with toasted sesame seeds if desired. Bake at 350
degrees for 10 to 15 minutes or until crisp. Check
occasionally and turn chips over if the middle is not
cooking as fast as the outside.

The thinner the chips, the crispier they'll be. These chips
are similar to potato chips and very tasty.

Crackers & Pastas Corner

Sesame Wheat Crackers

1½ cups whole wheat flour
½ cup water (more if needed)
1/3 cup vegetable oil
1 tsp. salt
½ tsp. baking powder
1 tsp. caraway seeds
¼ cup sesame seeds

Combine all ingredients and mix thoroughly. Roll
dough out thin on a lightly floured surface. Cut shapes
with cookie cutters or cut into small squares with knife.
Prick crackers with a fork or toothpick and place on a
non-stick baking sheet. Bake about 10 minutes at 350
degrees or until lightly browned. Be careful not to over
bake.

Crackers & Pastas Corner

Soft Wheat Pretzels

1 pkg. active yeast
½ cup warm water
½ cup sugar
1½ tsp. salt
2 cups milk, scalded and cooled to room temperature
½ cup vegetable oil
3 cups whole wheat flour
2½ to 3 cups all-purpose flour
¾ tsp. baking powder
2 quarts boiling water with 3 Tbsp. salt added
1 egg white, slightly beaten
Kosher salt

In a large bowl, using a rubber spatula, dissolve yeast in warm water. Gently stir in sugar, the 1½ tsp. salt, cooled milk and oil. Using a wooden spoon, gradually mix in 1½ cups whole wheat flour and 1 cup of all-purpose flour. Cover and let rise in a warm place until bubbly, about 40 minutes. Sift 1½ cups whole wheat flour and mix into dough. Place on a floured surface and knead for 5 minutes or until dough is no longer sticky, adding a little more all-purpose flour as needed. Roll dough out into a 9 by 15 inch rectangle and cut into strips ½ inch wide by 9 inches long. Using the palm of your hands, roll each strip into a 20 inch long rope and twist into a pretzel shape. Using a slotted spoon, lower one pretzel at a time into salted boiling water. It will drop to the bottom and float to the top in about 2 seconds. Remove from water and place on a greased cookie sheet about ½ inch apart. Brush with beaten egg white and sprinkle with kosher salt. Bake at 400 degrees for 20 minutes or until golden brown.

Crackers & Pastas Corner

Sprouted Wheat Crackers

Recipe taken from the Dead Sea Scrolls

Grind in meat grinder or food chopper, 2 cups sprouted wheat. * (about ¼ inch long sprouts) Puree in blender. The mashed wheat can be flavored to make a sweet cracker by adding honey, brown sugar, or any sweetener you like and sprinkling with cinnamon. To make a savory cracker you may add garlic, onion, celery, or seasoned salt. Sesame seeds go well on the savory crackers also.

Spread mashed mixture about 1/8 inch thick on a well-greased non-stick baking sheet and bake for about 2 hours at 300 degrees. You may also spread the mixture on a greased flat wood surface and place out in the hot sun for about 2-3 hours until crunchy.

Wheat Paste Crackers

4 cups Whole-wheat flour
Water as needed
Salt to taste

Make a thick paste with above ingredients. Should be the same consistency of paper paste. Spread thinly on an ungreased baking sheet and bake at 350 degrees for 40-45 minutes. Break into desired size crackers.

Crackers & Pastas Corner

Sugar-free Wheat Thins

1 ¾ cups whole wheat flour
1 ½ cups all-purpose flour
1/3 cup vegetable oil
¾ tsp. salt
1 cup water

In large bowl combine flours. Blend together the water, oil and salt and add to flour mixture. Mix well, but as little as possible. Roll out to 1/8 inch thick on an ungreased baking sheet. Score dough with knife for size crackers desired, do not cut through. Prick each cracker with fork 2-3 times and sprinkle with kosher, sea or seasoned salt. Bake for about 30 minutes at 350 degrees until lightly browned being careful not to over bake.

Crackers & Pastas Corner

Wheat Thins

1 cup whole wheat flour
1 cup all-purpose flour
½ cup sugar
¼ tsp. salt
2 Tbsp. soften butter <u>or</u> margarine
Approximately 2/3-cup milk
Kosher or sea salt for tops (optional)

Preheat oven to 325 degrees

Combine flours, sugar and salt in large mixing bowl.
Cut in butter until the mixture resembles a course meal.
Slowly blend in milk, using just enough to form a ball
that holds together.

Divide the dough in half and roll each portion out to
1/16-1/8 inch thick on a floured surface. Lightly
sprinkle with salt and gently roll over dough with rolling
pin. Using a sharp knife, cut crackers into 2 inch
squares. Place on ungreased cookie sheet. Prick
crackers 2-3 times with a fork and bake for 20 to 25
minutes or until lightly browned. Cool on a rack.

This recipe makes about 100 crackers.

Crackers & Pastas Corner

Whole wheat Crackers

4 cups whole wheat flour
2 tsp. plain or seasoned salt
2/3 cup powdered milk
1 Tbsp. honey
1 Tbsp. yeast
1 cup warm water
1/3 cup vegetable oil
½ cup warm water (may need more)
Sesame seeds (optional)

Combine dry ingredients in large bowl. Dissolve honey
and yeast in 1 cup warm water. Add yeast and honey
mixture, oil and ½ cup warm water to dry ingredients
and mix to form a ball of dough. Place dough into a
greased bowl, cover and let rise for ½-1 hour. Knead for
3 minutes and return to bowl. Using a piece of dough
the size of a lemon at a time, (cover remaining dough in
bowl) roll out on lightly floured surface. Roll each piece
as thin as possible and sprinkle with sesame seeds. Bake
on ungreased baking sheet for 6 minutes at 350 degrees.
Turn crackers over and bake another 2-3 minutes.
Watch them very carefully so not to over bake.
Cool on warm spot on top of stove.

Break by hand into irregular shaped crackers. Kids
enjoy this part.

Crackers & Pastas Corner

Whole Wheat Dumplings

2/3 cup whole wheat flour
1 tsp. baking powder
¼ tsp. salt
1 Tbsp. chopped fresh parsley (or 1 ½ tsp. dried)
¼ tsp. basil, thyme or dill weed
¼ cup milk
2 Tbsp. vegetable oil

Blend together the dry ingredients. Mix together and
pour milk and oil into flour mixture. Stir with a fork
until well combined. Drop with a tablespoon into
simmering soup or stew. Cook for 10 to 12 minutes or
until a toothpick comes out clean

Crackers & Pastas Corner

Whole Wheat Graham Crackers

½ cup evaporated milk
½ cup water
2 Tbsp. lemon juice
1-cup dark brown sugar
½ cup honey
6 cups whole-wheat flour (Approx.)

1 cup vegetable oil
2 tsp. vanilla
2 beaten eggs
1 tsp. salt
1 tsp.baking soda

In small bowl blend first 3 ingredients. In large bowl beat well the next 5 ingredients. Combine these two mixtures together and add the salt, soda and whole wheat flour. Divide dough into 4 parts. Place each on a greased and floured baking sheet and roll out to 1/8 inch thick. Prick with fork and bake at 375 degrees for about 15 minutes or until lightly brown. Immediately cut into desired size squares.

The kids are sure to love these healthy treats.

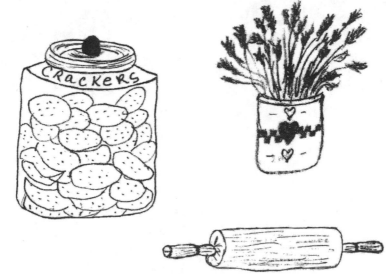

Crackers & Pastas Corner

Wonderful Whole Wheat Pasta

1 ¾ cups whole wheat flour
¼ cup toasted wheat germ
2 large eggs
3 to 6 Tbsp. water

Add whole wheat flour into a large mixing bowl and make a well in the center. Slightly beat eggs with 2 Tbsp. water then pour into well. Using a fork, gradually incorporate the flour into the egg mixture using a circular motion. Add 1 Tbsp. water and continue mixing. You may add more water, a little at a time, until flour is moistened
When dough becomes too stiff, finish mixing with your hands. Shape into a ball and let rest a few minutes to allow flour to absorb liquid. Place on floured surface and knead for 10 minutes or until smooth and elastic. Cover and let rest for 20 minutes.

Divide dough in 4 pieces and roll out one at a time to desired thickness. Always keep unrolled portions covered. When all dough has been rolled out, using a pastry cutter or sharp knife, cut into desired pasta shapes.
This recipe is perfect for lasagna, linguine, Fettuccini or spaghetti noodles.

To cook: Drop into salted boiling water for 8 to 10 minutes or until desired tenderness.

Dessert Corner

Dessert Corner

All-American Apple Pie

6 to 8 granny smith or pippin apples
1 Tbsp. lemon juice
1 cup sugar
3 to 3 ½ Tbsp. flour
1 ½ tsp. ground cinnamon
¼ tsp. ground nutmeg
¼ tsp. salt
2 Tbsp. butter

Prepare pastry for a 9"- double-crust pie (see pie crust recipe in this section)
Wash, core, peel and thinly slice apples. Turn into bowl and drizzle with lemon to prevent discoloration. Toss lightly with mixture of sugar, flour, cinnamon, nutmeg and salt. Pour mixture into unbaked pie shell and dot with butter. Complete as for a 2-crust pie.

Bake at 450 degrees for 10 minutes; reduce oven temperature 350 degrees and bake about 40 minutes or until crust is lightly browned.

Serve warm or cold with ice cream or a slice of cheddar cheese.

I LOVE MY COUNTRY

Dessert Corner

Apple & Pecan Cake

1 ½ cup vegetable oil
2 cups packed dark brown sugar
1 ½ tsp. vanilla
3 eggs
3 cups sifted whole-wheat pastry flour
1 tsp. salt
1 tsp. baking soda
3 large grated apples, peeled and cored
1 cup chopped pecan or walnuts
½ cup light brown sugar mixed with ½ tsp. cinnamon

Preheat oven to 350 degrees.

Cream together oil, dark brown sugar and vanilla. Beat
in eggs, one at a time, until well blended. Sift together
flour, salt and soda. Gradually add to oil mixture,
stirring until well blended. Fold in apples and nuts.
Pour batter in a greased 9"x13" baking dish and bake for
60 to 70 minutes.

In the last five minutes of baking, sprinkle with light
brown sugar and cinnamon mixture.

This wonderful and moist cake is especially good when
served with either whipped cream or ice cream. Enjoy!

WHEAT

Applesauce/Cinnamon Cookies

1 ½ cup butter-flavored shortening
1 cup packed brown sugar
1 egg
1 ½ cup applesauce
2 cups sifted whole wheat pastry flour
1 tsp. salt
½ tsp. baking soda
1 ½ tsp. cinnamon
1 cup quick oats
1 cup raisins
1 cup chopped walnuts

Preheat oven to 375 degrees.

Cream together butter and sugar; blend in egg and applesauce. Sift together the dry ingredients and add to creamed mixture. Blend well. Stir in oats, raisins and nuts. Chill for 30 minutes. Drop by heaping teaspoonful onto a greased baking sheet. Bake for 12 to 15 minutes.

Makes about 5 dozen.

Dessert Corner

Aunt Thursa's Bottled Fruit Cake

1 quart blended with juice (any fruit will do)
1-cup oil
2 cups sugar
4 cups whole-wheat flour
1 tsp. salt
4 tsp. baking soda
4 tsp. cinnamon
1 tsp. each nutmeg and cloves
2- cups nuts, raisins, dates <u>or</u> coconut. (Add 1 or
mix and match)

Preheat oven to 350 degrees.

Use fruit that has been sitting at room temperature. In a
large mixing bowl, blend fruit, sugar and oil. Sift dry
ingredients together and add to fruit mixture. Pour into a
greased and floured, 9"x13" pan. Bake for 40 to 45
minutes. Cool. For a decorative look, lay a paper doily
on top of cake and sprinkle with confectioner's sugar.
Lift off doily carefully.

This is pretty cake to serve with Sunday dinner.

From a friend

Baked Wheat Pudding

6 eggs
¾ cup brown sugar
½ tsp. salt
1 ½ tsp. vanilla
3 cups milk
2 cups cooked whole or cracked wheat
1-cup raisins

Beat eggs slightly. Add brown sugar, salt and vanilla.
Add milk and stir until all the sugar is dissolved. Add
wheat and stir to break up large lumps. Stir in raisins.
Pour into a well-greased 2-quart casserole dish. Sprinkle
with nutmeg or cinnamon and bake at 350 degrees for 1
hour or until set. Serve warm or cold. Top with cream,
fruit or whipped cream.

This is a twist on the bread pudding your grandma use to
make. It's great for breakfast on a cold winter's morning.

From a dear friend: Sandy Phelps

103

Dessert Corner

Banana Nut Cake

½ cup butter <u>or</u> margarine
2 eggs
1 tsp. soda
1 cup sugar
2 cups whole wheat pastry flour
3 ripe bananas, mashed
4 Tbsp. sour cream
2/3 cup chopped walnuts

Preheat oven to 375 degrees.

In a large mixing bowl, combine all ingredients and mix until well incorporated. Pour into a greased and floured 9"x 13" baking pan. Bake for 25 to 30 minutes. Frost with caramel frosting. (See cake and cookies corner.) This is a banana lover's dream; rich and moist.

Yummy!

The Best Carrot Cake

2 cups sugar
4 eggs
1 ½ vegetable oil
2 cups shredded carrots
1 2-lb. can crushed pineapple
1 ½ tsp. vanilla
1 ½ cups whole wheat flour
1 cup all-purpose flour
2 tsp. baking powder
1 ½ tsp. salt
1 cup chopped walnuts

Preheat oven to 350 degrees

Combine sugar, eggs and oil in large mixing bowl. Add carrots, pineapple and vanilla and blend well. Blend in flours, baking soda and salt. Stir in walnuts. Grease and lightly flour 2-9" rounds or a 9"x13" cake pan. Pour batter into pans and bake for 35 to 40 minutes for rounds or 45 to 50 minutes for 9"x13". Cool on wire racks. Frost with cream cheese frosting. This is a moist and delicious cake.

<u>**Cream cheese frosting**</u>: 6-oz. cream cheese, ½ cup butter, 2-tsp. vanilla and 4 ½ to 4 ¾ cups sifted powdered sugar.
Blend cream cheese, butter and vanilla together well. Gradually add in powdered sugar to make frosting to spreading consistency.

Dessert Corner

Carolyn's Yummy Vanilla Cream Pie Filling

1 sugar	4 egg yolks
½ cup all-purpose flour	3 Tbsp. butter
¼ tsp. salt	1½ tsp. vanilla
3 cups milk	1-9" pastry shell

In a medium saucepan, combine sugar, flour and salt. Gradually stir in milk with wooden spoon or wire whip. Cook and stir continually over medium heat until mixture thickens and is bubbly. Reduce heat, cook and stir for 2 minutes. Remove from heat. Slightly beat egg yolks and gradually stir 1 cup of hot mixture into yolks. Add egg mixture to sauce pan and bring to gentle boil. Cook and stir 2 minutes more. Remove from heat and stir in butter and vanilla. Pour filling into baked pastry shell. Cover with Plastic wrap to prevent a skin from forming. Allow to cool to room temperature for 4 to 6 hours and refrigerate. May be topped with meringue or Carolyn prefers fresh sweetened whipped cream with a dash of vanilla.

Coconut Cream Pie: Add 1 cup flaked coconut with vanilla and sprinkle whipped cream with 1/3 cup flaked coconut.

Banana Cream Pie: Slice 3 bananas to bottom of pastry crust before adding your filling. Top with sweetened whipped cream.

Chocolate Cream Pie: Decrease sugar to ¾ cup and add 3 ounces chopped semi-sweet chocolate when adding milk. Top with sweetened whipped cream.

From a dear friend: Carolyn Sandoval

I LOVE MY COUNTRY

Dessert Corner

Cherry Cobbler Bars

1 cup butter
1 ¾ cups sugar
4 eggs
1 tsp. almond <u>or</u> vanilla extract
2 cups all-purpose flour
1 cup whole wheat flour
¼ tsp. salt
1 ½ tsp. baking powder
1-16 oz. can cherry pie filling.

Powder sugar glaze: 1 cup powdered sugar, ½ tsp. Vanilla and 1 to 2 Tbsp. milk. Stir together until right consistency to drizzle.

Cream together butter and sugar. Add eggs and extract. Blend well. Add dry ingredients to butter mixture and mix together completely. Pour 2/3 of batter into a greased 11"x17" jelly roll pan. Spread on pie filling. Drop remaining batter by tablespoons onto pie filling. Bake at 350 degrees for 30 to 40 minutes. Cool slightly, then drizzle glaze over top of bars. Let cool and cut into desired size bars. You may use any pie filling you like.

I LOVE MY COUNTRY

Chocolate-Coconut Wheat Berry Candy

3 Tbsp. cocoa
½ cup milk
2 cups sugar
¼ tsp. salt
1 tsp. vanilla
1 cup cooked wheat berries
2 cups quick oaks
½ cup shredded coconut

In a small saucepan, stir together cocoa, milk, sugar, salt and vanilla. Stirring constantly, slowly bring a boil. Remove from heat and mix in wheat berries, oats, and coconut. Drop by teaspoonsful onto a greased cookie sheet or a piece of waxed paper. Put in refrigerator to set.

Yields: 30 pieces

I LOVE MY COUNTRY

Crunchy Peanut Butter Bars

½ cup sugar
¾ cup brown sugar
1 egg
½ cup butter
½ cup crunchy peanut butter
1-cup whole-wheat flour
1-cup quick oats
½ tsp. baking soda
½ tsp. salt

Preheat oven to 350 degrees

Combine all ingredients and blend well. Spread into a 9"x13" greased baking pan. Bake for 17 to 22 minutes until golden brown. Cool and frost with your favorite butter cream frosting. Cut into 1½-inch squares.

Variation: Sprinkle with 6 oz. pkg. of chocolate, peanut butter or butterscotch chips as soon as you remove pan from oven. Let set a few minutes and spread over bars

Yields about 4 dozen

I LOVE MY COUNTRY

Cullen Family's Frosted Irish Cake

2/3 cup butter
2 cups brown sugar
4 eggs, beaten
2 ¾ cups whole wheat flour
2 ½ tsp. baking powder
1 tsp. ground nutmeg
1 tsp. salt
1 cup milk
½ Tbsp. powdered cardamom
½ Tbsp. poppy seeds
½ Tbsp. anise seeds

In a large bowl, cream together butter, sugar, and eggs. Sift together the flour, baking powder, nutmeg and salt. Add to creamed mixture, alternating with the milk. Blend thoroughly. Pour 1/3 of mixture into a well-greased angel food cake pan. Combine the cardamom and seeds and sprinkle over batter. Pour the rest of the batter into pan and bake for 1 hour in a 350-degree oven. Allow to stand for 10 minutes after removing from oven. Using a sharp knife, loosen cake from sides of pan and remove cake from pan. Turn up side down on a plate and frost with Burnt butter frosting.

Burnt Butter Frosting: ¼ cup <u>real butter,</u> 1 lb. powder sugar, 4 or 5 Tbsp. water and 1 tsp. vanilla. Melt butter in a saucepan and cook until it becomes a rich brown color. Add the rest of the ingredients and mix until smooth. May add more water if too thick to spread.

Dessert Corner

Fake Date Cake

1 ½ cup sugar
2 cups whole wheat flour
1-tsp. baking powder
1 tsp. baking soda
1 tsp. cinnamon
1 tsp. nutmeg
1 tsp. allspice
¼ tsp. ground cloves
½ tsp. salt

1 tsp. vanilla
1 cup buttermilk
3 eggs
1 cup vegetable oil
1 cup minced cooked
 prunes
1 cup chopped walnuts

Sift together dry ingredients into a large mixing bowl. Add all remaining ingredients and mix together thoroughly. Pour into a 9"x 13" baking pan and bake at 350 degrees for 40 to 35 minutes. Cool slightly and drizzle with a lemon or orange glaze. (See frosting section)

Serves 15

From a dear friend: Sandy Phelps

WHEAT

Dessert Corner

Frosted German Chocolate Bars

2¼ cups whole-wheat pastry flour
¼ cup cornstarch
1/3 powdered milk
1 t sp. baking soda
½ cup water
1 pkg. German sweet chocolate
2 egg yolks
1-cup butter
1 Tbsp. vinegar
½ cup water

Sift together the flour, cornstarch, powdered milk, baking soda. Break chocolate bar into pieces and drop onto ½ cup boiling water to soften. In a large bowl, cream butter, sugar and egg yolks. Add vinegar and water with chocolate and blend well. Stir in sifted flour mixture and blend for 5 minutes. Pour out on a 12"x 17" baking sheet that has been lightly greased. Bake for 40 minutes at 350 degrees. Cool completely and frost with coconut frosting. Cut into 2-inch squares.

Coconut Frosting

1-cup sugar	7 oz pkg. coconut
3-egg yolks	½ cup chopped nuts
¾ cup evaporated milk	¼ cup butter

To blender, add sugar, egg yolks and milk. Liquify. Pour into a small saucepan. Add butter and bring to boil stirring constantly. Stir in coconut and nuts and blend well.

I LOVE MY COUNTRY

Fruit & Spice Cupcakes

1 cup chopped and pitted dates or prunes
1 cup boiling water
2 cups whole wheat pastry flour
1 ½ cup brown sugar
1 tsp. salt
1 ¼ tsp. baking soda
1 tsp. each allspice, cinnamon, nutmeg, cloves & ginger
½ cup oil
3 egg, slightly beaten
1 cup raisins

Pour boiling water over fruit and let stand for 2 hours.
In a large mixing bowl, stir together all remaining
ingredients. Pour undrained fruit into flour mixture.
Beat with electric mixer for 1 minute on low and 2
additional minutes on medium, scraping down sides of
bowl frequently. Lightly grease muffin cups or line with
paper bake cups. Fill ¾ full and bake at 350 degrees for
25 minutes. Frost with butter cream frosting. (See in
frosting section)

Makes about 30 cupcakes

Dessert Corner

Gingerbread People Cookies

½ cup shortening
½ cup sugar
½ cup dark molasses
1 Tbsp. cider vinegar
1 tsp. vanilla
3 cups sifted whole-wheat pastry flour
1 tsp. baking soda
½ tsp. salt
1 tsp. cinnamon
1 Tbsp. ginger
½ tsp. cloves
½ cup hot water

In a large bowl, cream together shortening and sugar. Add molasses, vinegar and vanilla and blend well. Stir dry ingredients together. Add flour mixture into creamed mixture, alternating with the hot water until all the flour is incorporated into the dough. Divide dough in half; wrap in plastic wrap and chill for 2 hours. On a lightly floured surface, roll out half of the dough at a time, ¼ inch thick. Cut with 4 ½ to 6-inch people cookie cutters. Place 1 inch apart on a greased cookie sheet. Bake at 350 degrees for 8 to 10 minutes or until set. Cool on a wire rack.
Decorate with icing and decorative candies. Raisins and chocolate chips work great for eyes and buttons.

Makes 36 to 48

I LOVE MY COUNTRY

Glazed Soft Sugar Cookie

1 cup sour cream
1 tsp. cider vinegar
2 eggs
¾ cup butter
1 ¾ cups sugar
1 ½ tsp. vanilla
2 tsp. baking soda
3 to 4 cups all-purpose flour
2 to 2 ½ cups whole wheat pastry flour

Stir sour cream and vinegar together and set aside. In a large mixing bowl, blend rest of ingredients except for the flours. Add sour cream mixture. Blend in the flours gradually until dough is workable. Roll out on a lightly floured surface to ¼ " thick. Cut with floured cookie cutter. Cook on a greased cookie sheet at 375 degrees for 8 minutes. Transfer to wire racks and spread with lemon or orange glaze while cookies are still warm.

Glaze: 1 ¼ cups powdered sugar, ¼ cup lemon or orange juice and 1 tsp. vanilla. Mix until smooth.

From a dear friend: Sandy Phelps

I LOVE MY COUNTRY

Golden Apple Brown Betty

8-large granny smith apples (peeled, cored and thinly sliced.)
¾ cup undiluted apple juice concentrate
½ cup raisins
2/3 cup whole wheat flour
1 ½ tsp. cinnamon
½ cup quick oats
¼ cup sliced walnuts
3 Tbsp. brown sugar
3 Tbsp. melted butter

Preheat oven to 350 degrees

In a large bowl, combine apples, apple juice concentrate, raisins, 3 Tbsp. flour and cinnamon. Pour into 9" x 11" baking dish. Stir together remaining flour, oats, nut and brown sugar. Add melted butter and mix until crumbly. Sprinkle crumb mixture over apples and bake for 1 hour or until apples are tender and the top is golden.

Serve hot or cold. Ice cream is wonderful on top of this fruity dessert.

I LOVE MY COUNTRY

Dessert Corner

Great Oatmeal and Raisin Cookies

1 cup butter-flavored shortening
1 cup brown sugar-packed
2 beaten eggs
2 ¼ cups sifted whole wheat flour
1 tsp. baking soda
½ salt
1 tsp. each cinnamon and nutmeg
¾ cup milk
2 cups quick oats
1 cup raisins
1 cup chopped nuts (optional

Preheat oven to 350 degrees

In a large mixing bowl, cream together shortening and sugar. Beat in eggs. Sift flour, salt and spice together twice. Add flour and milk alternately to creamed mixture; blend well between each addition. Stir in oats, raisins and nuts. Drop by heaping teaspoonfuls onto a greased cookie sheet and bake for 17 to 20 minutes.

You may add chocolate chips if desired.

Make about 3 ½ dozen

I LOVE MY COUNTRY

Dessert Corner

Gumdrop Bars

2 eggs
1-cup sugar
1 ½ tsp. vanilla
1 cup sifted whole-wheat flour
½ tsp. salt
2/3-cup miniature gumdrops (or cut up regular size) do not use the black ones
½ cup chopped walnuts or pecans

WHEAT

Preheat oven to 325 degrees.

Beat eggs until foamy. Beat in the sugar and vanilla. Sift together flour and salt and stir into egg mixture. Add gumdrops and nuts. Mix together well. Spread into a well-greased 9"x9" inch cake pan. Bake for 30 to 35 minutes. The top will crack slightly, but the inside will still be moist when done.

Cut into squares while still warm. Let cool completely, and then remove from pan.

From a dear friend: Sandy Phelps

Homemade Wheat Brownies

1 cube butter – melted
¼ cup cocoa
1 cup sugar
2 eggs
½ tsp. salt
½ tsp. baking powder
1 tsp. vanilla
1 cup whole wheat flour
½ cup chopped pecans, walnuts, or almonds

Melt butter in microwave and add remaining ingredients
one at a time, beating after each addition with the exception
of the nuts. Stir nuts in last. Pour batter into greased 8" x 8"
pan and bake at 350 degrees for 25 minutes. This recipe
can be doubled and put into a 9" x 13" pan.

Yummy

I LOVE MY COUNTRY

Martha Washington's Cherry Pie

Prepare pastry for an 8"double crust pie. (See pie crust recipe in this section)

1 cup sugar
2 ½ Tbsp. cornstarch
¼ salt
2 cans (16 oz. each) pitted tart red cherries, drain and reserve ¾ cup liquid
1 tsp. fresh lemon juice
¼ tsp. almond extract
1 Tbsp. butter

Combine sugar, cornstarch and salt in a heavy saucepan; stir in reserved cherry liquid. Bring to a boil and continue to let boil for 3 minutes, stirring constantly. Remove from heat; stir in lemon juice, almond extract and cherries. Set aside and let cool completely. Spoon cooled filling into unbaked pastry shell and dot with butter. Complete as for a 2-crust pie.

Bake at 450 degrees for 10 minutes; reduce oven temperature to 350 degrees and bake about 35 minutes, or until lightly brown. Remove pie to wire rack to cool.

Serve warm or cold. Wonderful with a big scoop of vanilla ice cream.

Nutmeg Cake

¼ cup butter or margarine	1 tsp. baking soda
¼ cup shortening	1 tsp. baking powder
1-½ cups sugar	2-tsp. nutmeg
1 tsp. vanilla	¼ tsp. salt
3 eggs	1 cup buttermilk
1-cup whole wheat pastry flour	1 cup all-purpose flour

Preheat oven to 350 degrees.

Cream first 4 ingredients together. Beat in eggs. Sift together flour, soda, baking powder, nutmeg and salt. Add to butter mixture, alternating with buttermilk. Pour into greased 9"x 13" baking pan and bake for 30 minutes. Let cool.

This moist cake is wonderful dusted with powdered sugar and serve with a scoop of ice cream. You may frost it with a butter cream frosting if you prefer.

Dessert Corner

Old fashion Berry Cobbler

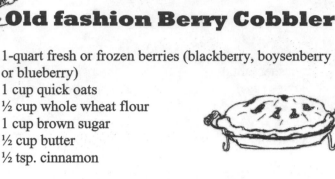

1-quart fresh or frozen berries (blackberry, boysenberry or blueberry)
1 cup quick oats
½ cup whole wheat flour
1 cup brown sugar
½ cup butter
½ tsp. cinnamon

Combine oats, flour, brown sugar and cinnamon in a bowl. Cut in butter until crumbly. Press 2/3 of mixture into the bottom of a greased 8"x 8" pan. Layer with berries. Crumble remaining mixture over berries. Bake at 350 degrees for 45 minutes or until brown and bubbly. If using frozen berries, allow additional baking time.

Serve warm or cold. It's nice with a little fresh cream poured on top or use whipped cream if you prefer.

Makes 9 servings

Dessert Corner

Old Woman in the Shoe Cookies

1 cup butter
1 cup sugar
1 cup brown sugar, packed
2 eggs
2 tsp. vanilla
2 cups whole wheat flour
2 tsp. baking soda
1 ½ tsp. baking powder
1 tsp. salt

Any or all of the following:

1 cup quick oats
1 cup rice cereal
1 cup shredded coconut
1 cup raisins

1 cup chocolate,
peanut butter or
butterscotch chips
1 cup nuts

Preheat oven to 350 degrees.

Cream butter until fluffy. Add sugars, eggs and vanilla and mix well. Combine flour, baking soda, baking powder and salt then add to the butter mixture. Stir in the other ingredients you've chosen and blend well. Drop by teaspoonful onto an ungreased cookie sheet. Bake for 10 minutes or until lightly browned. Allow the cookies to set a few minutes before removing from the cookie sheet.

I LOVE MY COUNTRY

Dessert Corner

Our Basic Chocolate Chip Cookie

1 cup butter-flavored shortening
¾ cup sugar
¾ cup brown sugar (packed)
2 eggs
2 Tbsp. hot water
1 ½ tsp. vanilla
½ tsp. salt
1 tsp. baking soda
1 ½ cups whole wheat pastry flour
1 cup all-purpose flour
1 cup chopped walnuts or pecans
1 pkg. 6 oz. chocolate chips

Preheat you oven to 350 degrees.

Combine shortening, sugars, eggs, hot water and vanilla. Blend well. Add salt, baking soda and both flours and blend until all flour has been incorporated into creamed mixture. Stir in chips and nuts and mix well. Using your hands, roll 1-½ teaspoonsful of dough into a ball and place on a greased cookie sheet 2-inches apart. Bake for 12 to 15 minutes. Cool on a wire rack.

These cookies may also be dropped by teaspoonful onto a greased cookie sheet.

Makes about 3 ½ dozen

I LOVE MY COUNTRY

Pam's Hubby's Favorite Snicker Doodle Cookie

1 cup butter (No substitutions)
1 ½ cup sugar
2 eggs
2 cups all-purpose flour
¾ cup whole wheat pastry flour
2 tsp. cream of tartar
1 tsp. baking soda
1 tsp. salt
2 cups chocolate chips

Preheat oven to 375 degrees

A Favorite !

In a large bowl, cream together well, butter, sugar and eggs. Add dry ingredients and blend until all the flour mixture is incorporated into the creamed mixture. Stir in chocolate chips. Bake for 8 to 10 minutes. The cookies will not look done, but remove from the oven and leave them on the cookie sheet for two minutes to finish cooking. Transfer to a wire rack to cool.

These cookies are wonderful! My husband can't get enough of them. They rarely make it to the cookie jar.

Makes about 3 dozen

I LOVE MY COUNTRY

125

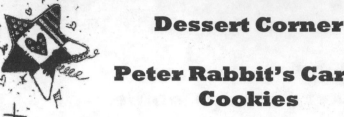

Peter Rabbit's Carrot Cookies

¾ cup sugar
¾ butter-flavored shortening
1 ½ tsp. vanilla
1 egg
1 cup shredded carrots
2 cups whole wheat pastry flour
1 tsp. baking powder
¼ tsp. salt

Cream together sugar and shortening until light and fluffy. Add vanilla and egg and beat well. Stir in shredded carrots. Combine flour, baking powder and salt; add to carrot mixture stirring until well blended. Drop by tablespoonful onto a greased cookie sheet. Bake for 10 minutes. Cool slightly on a wire rack, and then frost with orange glaze. (See recipe in frosting section.)

These are my kids' favorite.

From a dear friend: Joy Sides

I LOVE MY COUNTRY

Pooh-Bear Peanut Butter
N' Honey Cookies

1 cup peanut butter, creamy or crunchy
½ cup butter
½ cup honey
½ cup packed brown sugar
1 tsp. vanilla
1 egg
1 ½ cup whole-wheat pastry flour
½ tsp. baking powder
¾ tsp. baking soda
¼ tsp. salt

Thoroughly cream together the peanut butter, butter and honey. Add brown sugar gradually. Beat in vanilla and egg. Sift together the flour, baking powder, baking soda and salt. Add flour mixture into creamed mixture and blend well. Chill cookie dough for 30 minutes. Form into small balls. Place 2-inches apart on an ungreased cookie sheet. Flatten with a fork that has been dipped in granulated sugar to create a criss-cross pattern. Bake at 375 degrees for 10 to 15 minutes.

I LOVE MY COUNTRY

Prize Winning Sponge Cake

6 eggs, separated
1 tsp. cream of tartar
1 ½ cups sugar
½ tsp. vanilla
½ tsp. lemon extract
¼ tsp. almond extract
½ cup water
1 ½ cup whole wheat pastry flour
¼ tsp. salt

Preheat oven to 325 degrees

In a large mixing bowl, beat egg yolks and add sugar, extracts and water. Beat for 5 to 7 minutes until very thick and creamy. Sift whole wheat flour and salt twice. Gradually add flour to egg mixture beating continuously. Beat egg whites and cream of tartar until stiff peaks form. Immediately fold into batter. Pour into ungreased 10-inch tube pan and bake for 60 to 70 minutes or until top springs back when lightly touched. Remove from oven and immediately turn cake upside down. (Leave in pan) Cool thoroughly. Loosen sides of cake from pan; remove cake.

May be served plain or with fresh fruit and whipped cream.

Makes 12 servings

Dessert Corner

Pumpkin Chocolate Chip Cookies

1 ½ cups packed brown sugar
½ cup shortening
1 cup pumpkin
1 egg
1 tsp. vanilla
1 tsp. each of cinnamon <u>and</u> nutmeg
½ tsp. cloves
1 tsp. salt
1 tsp. each baking soda <u>and</u> baking powder
2 ½ cups whole wheat pastry flour
1- 6 oz. pkg. chocolate chips
½ cup chopped nuts (optional)

Preheat oven to 400 degrees

In large bowl, blend together sugar, shortening, pumpkin, egg and vanilla. Add spices, salt, baking powder, baking soda and flour. Blend until flour mixture is well incorporated. Stir in chocolate chips and nuts. Bake on greased cookie sheet for 10 to 12 minutes.

Makes 3 ½ to 4 dozen.

Quick to Make Chocolate Cake

1 ½ cup whole wheat flour
3 Tbsp. cocoa powder
1 tsp. baking soda
1 cup sugar
½ tsp. salt
5 Tbsp. vegetable oil
1 Tbsp. cider vinegar
1 tsp. vanilla
1 cup cold water

Into a large bowl, sift together dry ingredients. Add all remaining ingredients. Beat with a spoon until all lumps are gone and batter is smooth. Spray a 9"x 9" cake pan with cooking spray and pour in your batter. Bake at 350 degrees for 30 minutes. The kids love to help with this cake.

This moist cake needs no frosting, but is great, served with ice cream or warmed applesauce.

From a dear friend: Andrea Gouff

Quick to Make Danish Apple Pie

6 or 7 peeled and sliced granny smith or pippin' apples
¾ cup honey
1 cube butter
1 ½ cups whole-wheat pastry flour
1/8 tsp. salt
1 ½ tsp. cinnamon

Place apples in a buttered 9"x 13" baking dish and drizzle with honey. Cut butter into small pieces and combine together with flour, salt and cinnamon. You can mix this with a fork or use your hands. Sprinkle evenly over apples and bake for 45 minutes at 450 degrees.

This pie is wonderful with a big scoop of vanilla ice cream.

From a friend: Ruth Nelson

Yummy

I LOVE MY COUNTRY

Scrumptious Apple-Oatmeal Cake

1 ½ cup vegetable oil
2 cups packed dark brown sugar
1 ½ tsp. vanilla
3 eggs
3 cups sifted whole-wheat pastry flour
1 tsp. salt
1 tsp. baking soda
3 large grated apples, peeled and cored
1 cup chopped pecan or walnuts
½ cup light brown sugar mixed with ½ tsp. cinnamon

Preheat oven to 350 degrees.

Cream together oil, dark brown sugar and vanilla. Beat in eggs, one at a time, until well blended. Sift together flour, salt and soda. Gradually add to oil mixture, stirring until well blended. Fold in apples and nuts. Pour batter in a greased 9"x13" baking dish and bake for 60 to 70 minutes.

In the last five minutes of baking, sprinkle with light brown sugar and cinnamon mixture.

This wonderful moist cake is especially good when served with either whipped cream or ice cream. Enjoy!

Dessert Corner

Scrumptious Oatmeal Cake with Boiled Frosting

1 ½ cup boiling water
1 cup oatmeal, quick cooking
1 cup chopped raisins
½ cup vegetable shortening
1 cup brown sugar, packed
½ cup sugar
2 eggs, well beaten
1 ½ cups sifted whole wheat pastry flour
1/2 tsp. salt
1 tsp. baking soda
1 ½ tsp. cinnamon

A Favorite !

Preheat oven to 350 degrees.

Mix boiling water, oatmeal and raisins together and set aside to cool. In a large mixing bowl, cream together shortening, sugars and eggs. Sift together flour, salt, soda and cinnamon. Gradually add to creamed mixture, stirring until well blended. Add soaked oatmeal and mix together. Pour batter in a greased 9"x13" baking dish and bake for 45 to 55 minutes. Spread with boiled frosting while cake is still hot.

Boiled frosting: 1 cup butter, 1 cup brown sugar, 2 ½ Tbsp. cream or evaporated milk, ½ cup flaked coconut and ½ cup chopped nuts. Mix all together in small saucepan and boil for 2 minutes. Spread on cake. Yum!

This wonderful and moist cake is especially good when served with either whipped cream or ice cream. Enjoy!

I LOVE MY COUNTRY

133

Dessert Corner

Simple Simon Pie Crust
One & Two

No. 1

1 ½ cup whole wheat pastry flour
2 tsp. sugar
¾ tsp. salt
½ cup vegetable oil
2 Tbsp. <u>cold</u> milk

Sift directly into a pie pan, whole wheat pastry flour,
sugar and salt. Combine vegetable oil and milk in small
bowl and mix well with fork. Pour into pie pan and stir
with fork until all flour is moist. Mold dough with
fingers around pie pan to form a crust. Finish edge by
pressing tines of fork all around edge of crust. Bake as
directed for individual recipes.

No. 2

1 cube butter, softened
2 Tbsp. sugar
1 cup whole wheat pastry flour

Cream together butter and sugar. Using a fork, quickly
blend in flour and mold into pie pan with your fingers.
Bake at 325 for 12 minutes. Watch carefully, because it
browns very fast.

From a dear friend: Sandy Phelps

Sour Cherry Cookies

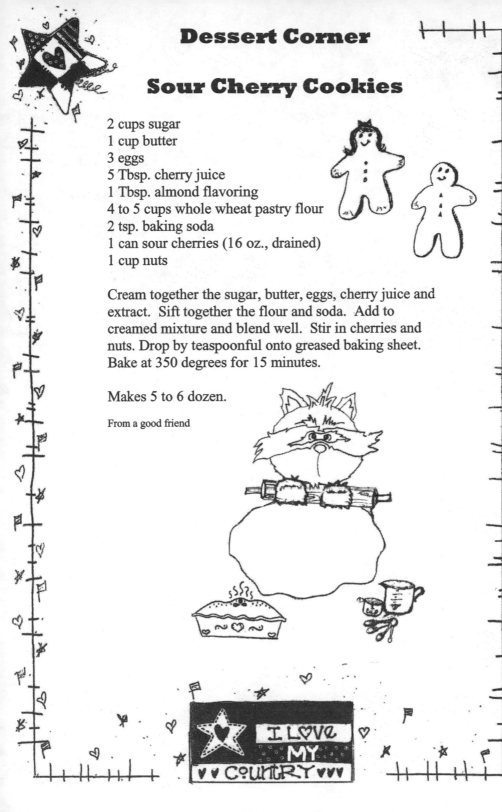

2 cups sugar
1 cup butter
3 eggs
5 Tbsp. cherry juice
1 Tbsp. almond flavoring
4 to 5 cups whole wheat pastry flour
2 tsp. baking soda
1 can sour cherries (16 oz., drained)
1 cup nuts

Cream together the sugar, butter, eggs, cherry juice and extract. Sift together the flour and soda. Add to creamed mixture and blend well. Stir in cherries and nuts. Drop by teaspoonful onto greased baking sheet. Bake at 350 degrees for 15 minutes.

Makes 5 to 6 dozen.

From a good friend

I LOVE MY COUNTRY

Sweet Potato Dump Cake

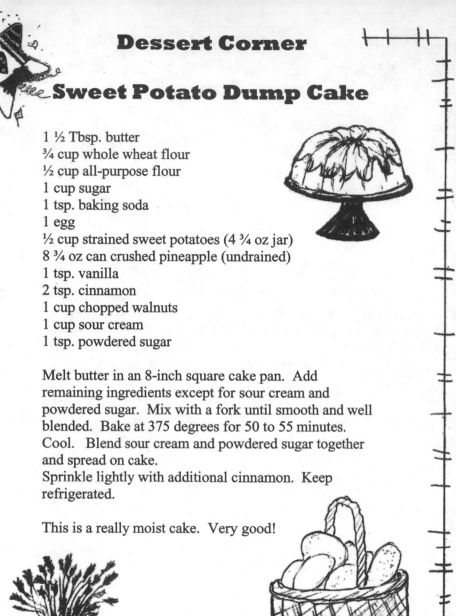

1 ½ Tbsp. butter
¾ cup whole wheat flour
½ cup all-purpose flour
1 cup sugar
1 tsp. baking soda
1 egg
½ cup strained sweet potatoes (4 ¾ oz jar)
8 ¾ oz can crushed pineapple (undrained)
1 tsp. vanilla
2 tsp. cinnamon
1 cup chopped walnuts
1 cup sour cream
1 tsp. powdered sugar

Melt butter in an 8-inch square cake pan. Add remaining ingredients except for sour cream and powdered sugar. Mix with a fork until smooth and well blended. Bake at 375 degrees for 50 to 55 minutes. Cool. Blend sour cream and powdered sugar together and spread on cake.
Sprinkle lightly with additional cinnamon. Keep refrigerated.

This is a really moist cake. Very good!

I LOVE MY ♥♥ COUNTRY ♥♥♥

Thumb Print Jam Cookies

½ cup butter
¼ cup brown sugar
1 egg yolk
1 tsp. vanilla
1 cup whole wheat pastry flour
¼ tsp. salt
1 cup finely chopped walnuts
½ cup of your favorite jam or preserves

Preheat oven to 375 degrees

Cream together butter, sugar, egg yolk and vanilla. Sift flour and salt and add to butter mixture. Blend well. Form dough into 1-inch ball; roll in slightly beaten egg white and then into nuts. Place on ungreased cookie sheet and bake for 5 minutes. Remove from oven and quickly press thumb into the center of the cookies. Return to oven and bake for 8 minutes longer or until edges are lightly browned. Cool cookies on a wire rack. Just before serving, fill center with your favorite jam or preserves

Makes about 40 cookies

From a dear friend: Jennifer Cragun. She often baked these pretty cookies with her grandmother.

Dessert Corner
Whole Wheat Cream Puffs

1 ½ cups water
¾ cup butter
½ tsp. salt
1 ½ cup whole wheat pastry flour
6 eggs

Bring water and butter to a boil in a 1½-qt. saucepan.
Combine salt and flour together, add all at once, stirring
vigorously to boiling butter water. Continue to cook
and stir until it forms a ball that doesn't separate.
Remove from heat. Cool for 10 minutes. Add eggs, one
at a time, beating with a wooden spoon after each
addition until smooth.
Drop by heaping tablespoonful onto greased baking
sheet. Bake at 400 degrees for 10 minutes. Lower oven
temperature to 325 and bake for another 15 to 20
minutes or until golden. Remove from oven. Turn oven
off and return puff to oven for 10 minutes to dry. Cool
on a wire rack. Split in half and remove any soft dough
from inside. Fill with cream puff filling. (Recipe below)

Chocolate Eclairs
Prepare above cream puff recipe. Form éclair by
dropping 2 Tbsp. of dough side by side, forming a strip
about 4 inches long, ¾ inch wide, and 1 inch high.
Bake, fill and top with chocolate glaze. (See frosting
section.)

Cream Puff Filling

Yummy

2 cups milk	2 eggs, beaten
¾ cup sugar	1 tsp. vanilla
1/8 tsp. salt	1 cup sweeten whipped cream

Scald milk. Mix sugar, flour and salt and add to milk.
Stir constantly over low heat until thickened. Cool over
hot water (not boiling) in a double boiler for 15 minutes.
Slowly add mixture to beaten eggs, stirring continually.
Return to double boiler and cook, stirring constantly for
4 minutes. Chill. Fold in whipped cream and vanilla. Fill
cream puffs.

I LOVE MY COUNTRY

Whole Wheat Devil's Food Cake
(Red Velvet)

½ cup butter
1 ½ cup sugar
2 eggs
1 oz. red food coloring
1 tsp. vanilla
2 ½ Tbsp. unsweetened cocoa
¼ cup cornstarch
1 ¾ cups whole wheat flour
½ tsp.salt
1 cup buttermilk
1 tsp. baking soda
1 tsp. vinegar

Cream together the butter, sugar, eggs, food coloring and vanilla in a large mixing bowl. Combine the cocoa, cornstarch, whole wheat flour and salt. Sift onto a sheet of parchment or wax paper. Beat into creamed mixture alternately with buttermilk. Add soda to vinegar (hold over bowl as it foams.) Blend with other mixture only enough to mix in. Pour into 2-9" round, greased and lightly floured cake pans. Bake for 30 to 35 minutes in a 350-degree oven. Cool on wire racks and frost with Creamy white frosting. (Recipe in frosting section)

I LOVE MY COUNTRY

Whole Wheat Pastry for Double Pie Crust

1 cup whole wheat flour
1 cup all-purpose flour
2/3 cup cold butter-flavored shortening
6 to 7 Tbsp. ice cold water

Combine flour and salt in large bowl. Cut in shortening with a pastry cutter until pieces are the size of small peas. Add 1 Tbsp. ice water and gently toss with a fork. Repeat this process until all the flour is moistened. Form into a ball. Place on a floured surface and flatten with the palm of your hand. Roll out from center to edges, forming a 12-inch circle. Wrap around a floured rolling pin and unroll onto pie pan, being careful not to stretch pastry. Trim pastry even with the rim of the pie pan. Fill with desired filling. Place top crust on filling and cut 5 to 6 –1" slits to allow steam to escape during baking. Trim off top crust ½" beyond edge of pie pan and fold under bottom crust, flute edge. Bake as directed for individual recipes.

Whole Wheat Single Pie Crust

½ cup whole wheat flour
¾ all-purpose flour
¼ tsp. salt
1/3 cup cold butter-flavored shortening
3 to 4 Tbsp. ice cold water

Combine flour and salt in bowl. Cut in shortening with a pastry cutter until pieces are the size of small peas. Add 1 Tbsp. of ice water and gently toss with a fork. Repeat this process until all the flour is moistened. Form dough into ball. Place on a floured surface and flatten with the palm of your hand. Roll out dough from the center to the edges, forming a 12" circle. Wrap pastry around a floured rolling pin and unroll onto pie pan. Ease pastry into pie pan being careful not to stretch it. Trim pastry 1/2 inch beyond edge of pie pan. Fold pastry under so that it's even with rim of pan and crimp between your thumb and index finger or use fork tines to finish off edge of crust.
Do not prick pastry. Bake as directed for your favorite pie recipe.

Whole Wheat Pineapple Upside Down Cake

2 cups sugar
2/3 cups softened butter
2 eggs
1 ½ tsp. vanilla
3 cups whole wheat flour
1 tsp. salt
3 tsp. baking powder
2 cups milk
1 1/2 Tbsp. brown sugar
1-20oz. can sliced pineapple drained, reserve juice.

Preheat oven to 350 degrees

Cream together sugar, softened butter, eggs and vanilla. Add dry ingredients and milk to creamed mixture and blend well. Sprinkles brown sugar into bottom of a 9"x13" pan and top with pineapple slices and 3 Tbsp. juice. Pour batter over pineapple and bake for 30 to 40 minutes. Remove from oven and turn out on a large platter.

142

Dessert Corner

Butter Cream Frostings

Basic Butter Cream Frosting

6 Tbsp. butter	4½ cups confectioners
1 ½ tsp. vanilla	¼ cup milk <u>or</u> cream

Cream butter and vanilla. Gradually beat in sugar 1 cup at a time, beating thoroughly after each addition. Stir in milk <u>or</u> cream and beat until frosting is of spreading consistency.

Chocolate Butter Frosting

Prepare as above, except beat in ½ cup unsweetened cocoa powder into butter and vanilla.

Lemon Butter Frosting

Follow the basic butter cream recipe substituting lemon juice for the milk. Add 1 ½ tsp. grated lemon peel. You may add a few drops of yellow food coloring if you desire.

Orange Butter Frosting

Follow the basic butter cream recipe substituting 2 ½ Tbsp. orange juice for the milk. Omit vanilla and add 1 ½ tsp. grated orange peel. For a deeper orange color, mix 4 drops of red and 3 drops of yellow food color with orange juice.

Peanut Butter Frosting

Follow the basic butter cream recipe substituting creamy peanut butter for butter.

I LOVE MY COUNTRY

Dessert Corner

Cocoa Peanut Butter Frosting

1 lb. box confectioner's sugar
½ cup unsweetened cocoa powder
¼ tsp. salt
1 tsp. vanilla
7 Tbsp. boiling water
6 Tbsp. butter or margarine, softened
3 Tbsp. peanut butter

In a medium bowl, combine sugar, cocoa powder and salt. Add boiling water and vanilla and mix well. Add butter or margarine and peanut butter and beat until smooth. Frosting thickens as it cools. If it becomes too thick, stir in a few drops of hot water.

Cream Cheese Frosting

8 oz. cream cheese
1 cube butter or margarine, softened
2 tsp. vanilla
4½ to 5 cups confectioner's sugar

Beat together cream cheese, butter or margarine, and vanilla till light and fluffy. Gradually add the confectioner's sugar 1 cup at a time until frosting is of spreading consistency.

Chocolate Cream Cheese Frosting

Follow cream cheese frosting recipe substituting ¼ cup unsweetened cocoa powder for ¼ cup confectioner's sugar.

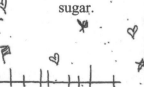

I LOVE MY COUNTRY

Creamy White Frosting

1 cup shortening
1 ½ tsp. vanilla
½ tsp. lemon, orange <u>or</u> almond extract
4 ½ cups sifted confectioner's sugar
3 to 4 Tbsp. milk

Beat shortening, vanilla and extract with an electric mixer on medium for 1 minute. Gradually add 2 cups of powdered sugar, beating well. Add 2 Tbsp. milk. Gradually beat in remaining sugar and just enough milk, 1 Tbsp. at a time until frosting is of spreading consistency.

Caramel Frosting

1 cup brown sugar
1/8 tsp. salt
1/3 cup milk
2 Tbsp. butter
1 tsp. vanilla
1 Tbsp. cream

In a small saucepan, over a medium heat, stir together the brown sugar, salt milk and butter. Cook stirring constantly until sugar dissolves. Continue cooking without stirring until mixture forms a softball stage. Cool to lukewarm. Beat until it begins to thicken. Add vanilla and cream. Continue beating until thick enough to spread. You may add a little powdered sugar at a time if needed.

This recipe frosts a 9"x 13" cake.

I LOVE MY COUNTRY

Dessert Corner

Sour Cream Chocolate Frosting

4 Tbsp. butter <u>or</u> margarine
1-cup semi-sweet chocolate chips
½ cup sour cream
2 ½ sifted powdered sugar

In a saucepan, melt butter and chips over low heat, stirring constantly. Cool 5 minutes. Stir in sour cream. Gradually add powdered sugar 1 cup at a time, beat till smooth and of spreading consistency. Store cake in refrigerator.

You may melt butter and chips in your microwave if you desire. Cook uncovered for 1 to 2 minutes or till softened, stirring once. Stir until smooth and let cool for 5 minutes.

Coconut-Pecan Frosting

1 egg
2/3 cup evaporated milk
2/3 cup sugar
4 Tbsp. butter <u>or</u> margarine
1 1/3 cups flaked coconut
2/3 cup chopped pecans

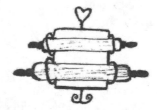

In a saucepan beat egg slightly. Stir in milk, sugar, and butter <u>or</u> margarine. Cook, stirring constantly, over medium heat 10 to 12 minutes or till thickened and bubbly. Stir in coconut and pecans. Allow to cool completely before spreading on cake.

146

Dessert Corner

Confectioner's Sugar Glazes

Vanilla Glaze

1 cup confectioner's sugar
¼ tsp. vanilla
Milk

Mix the sugar, vanilla and 1 Tbsp. of milk. Add additional milk, 1 Tsp. at a time, until desired consistency.
Makes ½ cup.

Chocolate glaze

Prepare as above, except add 2 Tbsp. unsweetened cocoa powder-to-powder sugar and stir together.

Orange or Lemon Glaze

Follow the recipe for vanilla glaze, using orange or lemon juice in place of milk.

Cooked Chocolate Glaze

½ cup semi-sweet chocolate chips
3 Tbsp. butter or margarine
1 ½ cup sifted confectioner's sugar

In a saucepan, melt chocolate chips and butter over low heat, stirring constantly. Remove from heat, stir in confectioner's sugar and 3 Tbsp. hot water. Stir in additional hot water, if needed, until desired consistency.

You may melt the chocolate and butter in your microwave
For 1 to 1 ½ minutes or until softened, stirring once. Stir till smooth and continue as above.

This frosting is perfect for spooning over a cake, allowing the excess to drizzle down the sides, or to top your eclairs or cream puffs.

Dessert Corner

Pam's Hints for Better Cake Baking

1. To use whole wheat in your favorite cake recipe, substitute approximately one-fourth of the amount of flour given in the recipe with cornstarch and use whole-wheat flour for the other three-fourths. This will give the cake a finer texture and help it keep its delicate lightness

2. To eliminate a course texture in a cake, be sure to beat it thoroughly together. Most cakes require that the batter is beaten about 300 strokes by hand or about 2 minutes with electric mixer after the last ingredients have been added. After the batter is poured into the pan, gently tap the pan on the countertop so the small bubbles will rise to the top. Break bubbles with a spoon and then bake as per recipe directions.

3. Is your cake done? Always check a cake by inserting a toothpick in the center of the cake. If it comes out clean, the cake is done. If the batter clings to the toothpick, bake the cake a little longer.

Grandma's
Sourdough Corner

Grandma's Corner

The Red White & Blue

Here it is the month of June,
The 4th of July will be coming soon!
What does the 4th of July mean to you,
When you pledge the red, white and blue?

Does it fill your soul with excitement and pride?
Do you feel it deep down inside,
And do you, when you see ol' glory waving high,
Think of all those men, who gave their lives,
And said, we will protect our country or die?

To think of the wonderful freedoms,
That's there for me and you,
That you are an American through and through.
Let's gird up our loins and be faithful and true,
To what it stands for, the Red, White and Blue.

This is a wonderful poem by Faye Crockett

Grandma Faye Crockett

24 Hour - Whole Wheat Sourdough Bread

Sourdough Starter:
¾ cup sourdough starter
¾ cup warm water
1 ½ cups whole wheat flour

Mix ingredients together in a glass or plastic bowl. Cover and let rest for 12-18 hours.

2 tsp. active dry yeast
½ cup warm water
2 cups whole wheat flour
2 ½ tsp. salt

Sprinkle the yeast onto the water and stir gently with a wooden spoon. (Not metal) In a large glass or plastic bowl, combine the flour and salt. Add the starter and yeast mixtures to flour and stir until it forms soft dough. Turn out onto a floured surface and knead for 10 minutes. Dough should be smooth and elastic. Add a little more flour at a time if needed. Place dough in a greased bowl, cover and let rise for 2 hours in a warm place.

Press dough flat and cut into 2 portions. Round portions and allow them to rest for 10 minutes. Shape into 2-8x4 inch loaves or 1 large round loaf. Preheat your oven to 375 degrees. Place your bread onto a baking sheet that has been lightly sprinkled with cornmeal. Bake for 45 to 50 minutes. Breads may be scored diagonally with a sharp knife before cooking if desired.

This recipe makes 2 loaves, 1 large round, 3 small rounds or 6 to 8 sandwich rounds.

Alaskan Outback Chocolate Cake

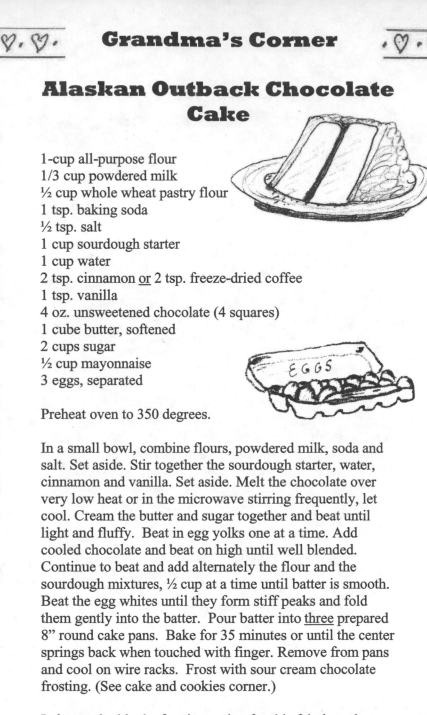

1-cup all-purpose flour
1/3 cup powdered milk
½ cup whole wheat pastry flour
1 tsp. baking soda
½ tsp. salt
1 cup sourdough starter
1 cup water
2 tsp. cinnamon <u>or</u> 2 tsp. freeze-dried coffee
1 tsp. vanilla
4 oz. unsweetened chocolate (4 squares)
1 cube butter, softened
2 cups sugar
½ cup mayonnaise
3 eggs, separated

Preheat oven to 350 degrees.

In a small bowl, combine flours, powdered milk, soda and salt. Set aside. Stir together the sourdough starter, water, cinnamon and vanilla. Set aside. Melt the chocolate over very low heat or in the microwave stirring frequently, let cool. Cream the butter and sugar together and beat until light and fluffy. Beat in egg yolks one at a time. Add cooled chocolate and beat on high until well blended. Continue to beat and add alternately the flour and the sourdough mixtures, ½ cup at a time until batter is smooth. Beat the egg whites until they form stiff peaks and fold them gently into the batter. Pour batter into <u>three</u> prepared 8" round cake pans. Bake for 35 minutes or until the center springs back when touched with finger. Remove from pans and cool on wire racks. Frost with sour cream chocolate frosting. (See cake and cookies corner.)

I always double the frosting recipe for this fabulous three-layered cake.

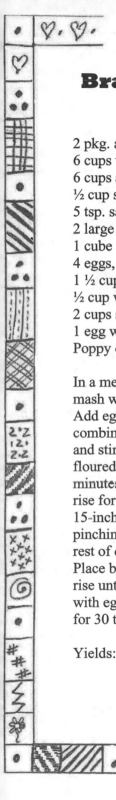

Braided Sourdough Potato Bread

2 pkg. active dry yeast
6 cups whole wheat pastry flour
6 cups all-purpose flour
½ cup sugar
5 tsp. salt
2 large russet potatoes
1 cube of butter
4 eggs, plus 1 yolk
1 ½ cups milk
½ cup water
2 cups sourdough starter
1 egg white beaten with 2 Tbsp. water (egg wash)
Poppy or sesame seeds (Optional.)

In a medium saucepan, cook potatoes until tender, drain and mash with butter. Stir in milk, water and sourdough starter. Add eggs and beat on high for 2 minutes. In a large bowl, combine yeast, flour, sugar and salt. Add potato mixture and stir until the dough is medium stiff. Turn out onto a floured surface and knead until smooth, about 8 to 10 minutes. Place in greased bowl, cover with a cloth and let rise for 2 hours. Divide into 12 balls. Roll each ball into a 15-inch long rope. Pinch 3 ropes together and loosely braid, pinching ends together and tuck underneath. Repeat with rest of dough.

Place braids on lightly greased baking sheets, cover and let rise until doubled. (About 45 minutes.) Brush loaves evenly with egg wash and sprinkle with seeds. Bake at 350 degrees for 30 to 35 minutes.

Yields: 4 braids

Easy Sourdough Crescent Rolls

**1-cup biscuit mix (wheat quick mix)
1/3-cup milk
1 Tbsp. sugar
½ tsp. soda
2 Tbsp. butter <u>or</u> margarine
½ cup sourdough starter
1 Tbsp. melted butter

Preheat oven to 400 degrees.

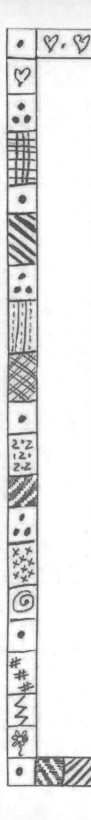

Combine biscuit mix, milk, sugar and soda. Cut in butter.
Add sourdough starter and stir just until blended. You may add more milk if needed. Turn out onto a floured surface and knead until no longer sticky. Divide dough in half and roll each half into a 9-inch circle. Brush with melted butter, then cut into 6 pie shaped wedges. Starting at wide end of wedge and roll into a crescent. Place on greased baking sheet and bake for 10 to 12 minutes.

Makes 12 crescent rolls.

**See the bread & biscuit corner for Wheat quick mix

158

Frosted Blonde Brownies

¼ cup butter
1 cup packed brown sugar
1 egg
1 tsp. vanilla
½ cup sourdough starter
1 cup all-purpose flour
½ cup baking soda
½ tsp. salt
½ cup chopped pecans
1-6 oz. pkg. chocolate or butterscotch chips

Preheat oven to 350 degrees.

Cream butter and sugar together. Beat in egg and vanilla until mixture is light and fluffy. Stir in sourdough starter. Sift flour, baking soda and salt onto a sheet of waxed paper. Add to sourdough mixture and blend well. Spread into a well-greased 8"x8" baking pan. Bake for 20 to 25 minutes or until surface springs back when touched with your finger. Be careful not to over bake! Sprinkle chips over top of hot brownies and let stand for 5 minutes. Spread melting chips over brownies to make frosting. Cut brownies while still warm.

This recipe makes 12 to 16 yummy brownies. Serve with a scoop of ice cream for a special treat.

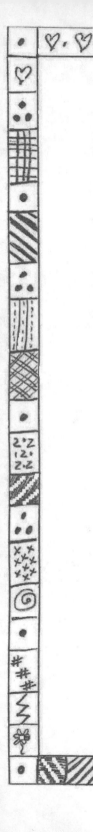

Honey Sourdough Bread

3 cups sourdough starter
2 Tbsp. dry milk
½ cup warm water
1½ Tbsp. honey
2 cups whole wheat flour.
2½ cups all-purpose flour
2 Tbsp. vegetable oil

In a large bowl, combine all ingredients except oil and mix well with a wooden spoon. Add oil and blend into flour mixture. Turn out onto a floured surface and knead for 10 minutes, or until dough is smooth and elastic. Place dough in a greased bowl, cover and let rise for 1 hour. Form into two loaves and place in greased bread pans. Cover with a damp cloth and let rise until doubled in size.

Preheat oven to 400 degrees. Bake for 30 minutes, reduce oven temperature to 325 and continue baking for 25 to 30 minutes.

This bread is wonderful toasted. Makes great turkey sandwiches too. My husband's favorite.

From a dear friend: Andrea Gouff

WHEAT

Multi-Grained Sourdough Bread

3 ½ cups warm water	1 cup cornmeal
2 Tbsp. active dry yeast	1 cup rye flour
1 cup sourdough starter `	1 cup wheat germ
1 1/3 cups rolled oats	1 cup soy flour
2 Tbsp. salt	¾ dry milk (Not instant)
1/3 cup molasses	5 cups whole-wheat flour
3 Tbsp. vegetable oil	

In a large glass or plastic bowl, sprinkle yeast into water and stir gently.   Add sourdough starter, oats, salt, molasses and oil. Stir until combined. Set aside for 10 to 12 minutes or until oats are softened.

Combine remaining ingredients and stir into oat mixture. Turn dough onto a floured surface and knead until dough is smooth and elastic. (About 10 minutes) If you need to add more whole wheat flour, be sure to add 2 Tbsp. of dry milk for every additional cup of flour added.

Place dough into a greased bowl, cover and let rise until doubled in size. Divide dough into 4 portions and shape into loaves. Place in greased bread pans, cover with a damp cloth, and let rise until doubled again.   Bake at 350 degrees for 35 to 40 minutes.

You'll love this hearty and healthy bread toasted with honey or as delicious French toast.

Makes 4 loaves

From a dear friend.

161

Sandy's Sourdough Coffee Cake

1-cup whole-wheat pastry flour
1-cup sourdough starter
¾ tsp. baking soda
¾ cup sugar
½ tsp. salt
½ tsp. cinnamon
1/3-cup vegetable oil
1 egg
1-cup raisins
½ cup chopped walnuts

Stir together all ingredients until well blended. Pour batter into a greased 8"x 8" pan. Prepare topping.

To prepare the topping, combine together the following ingredients:

1½ tsp. cinnamon
½ cup brown sugar, packed
1 Tbsp. flour
4 Tbsp. butter
1 Tbsp. sugar

Sprinkle batter with topping and bake at 350 degrees for 30 to 35 minutes.

Serve hot out of the oven and drizzle with melted butter.
Yummy!

Makes 6 to 9 servings.

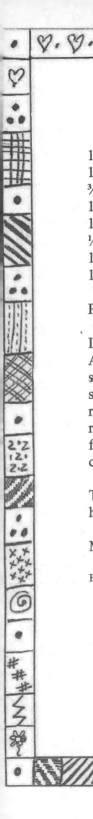

Soft Oatmeal & Raisin Cookies

1 cup butter-flavored shortening
1 cup sugar
¾ cup packed brown sugar
1 egg
1 tsp. vanilla
¼ cup water
1 cup sourdough starter
1 ½ cups whole wheat pastry flour

½ tsp. baking soda
1 tsp. salt
2 ½ cups quick oats
1 cup raisins
½ cup chopped walnuts
or pecans

Preheat oven to 400 degrees.

In a large bowl cream shortening and sugars together. Add eggs and vanilla, beat until fluffy. Stir in water and sourdough starter and set aside. Combine flour, baking soda and salt and stir into sourdough mixture. Add oats, raisins and nuts and stir until well incorporated. Drop by rounded teaspoonful onto a greased cookie sheet. Bake for 10 to 12 minutes or until golden brown. Transfer cookies to wire racks to cool.

This soft and moist cookie with a glass of cold milk is hard to beat for an afternoon snack.

Makes 3 to 4 dozen cookies.

From a dear friend: Joy Sides

Sourdough Biscuits

1 cup starter
1 tsp. soda
1 tsp. salt
1 tsp. sugar
1 Tbsp. vegetable shortening
2 ½ cups all-purpose flour
1 cup whole wheat flour

Preheat oven to 425 degrees.

Combine the flours in a large bowl. Make a well in the center and add starter. Stir in remaining ingredients. Gradually mix in more flour to make a stiff dough. Pinch off enough dough to form a ball. Roll each ball in melted butter and arrange in a cake pan. Let rise for 20 minutes. Bake for 12 to 15 minutes.

Enjoy these flavorful biscuits with lots of real butter and dripping with honey.

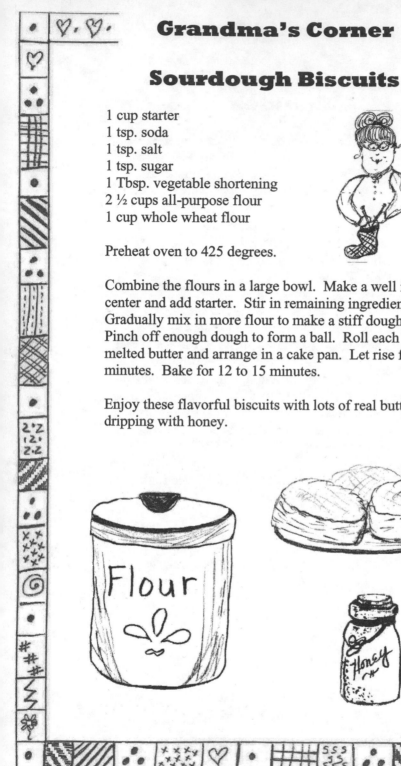

Sourdough Bread

1 pkg. active dry yeast
1 ½ cups warm water
1 cup sourdough starter
3 cups whole wheat flour
3 cups all-purpose flour
2 tsp. each of salt and sugar
½ tsp. soda

Sprinkle yeast over warm water in a large mixing bowl. Set aside while you measure 4 cups of the flour. Stir starter, 4 cups flour, salt and sugar into yeast and water. Stir vigorously with a large wooden spoon for 3-4 minutes. Place dough into a large greased bowl, cover with a towel, and let rise for 2 hours in a warm place. Combine baking soda with 1 cup of remaining flour and stir into dough.

Turn dough out onto a lightly floured surface. Knead in remaining flour until dough is smooth and not sticky, (about 8 to 10 minutes) you may add more flour if needed. Shape into 2 oblong loaves and place on a greased baking sheet, cover and let rise until doubled. Just before baking, brush loaves with water and score the tops diagonally 3 or 4 times with a sharp knife.

Preheat oven to 400 degrees. Place shallow pan of hot water in the bottom of oven, place bread in oven and bake for 45 to 50 minutes.

Makes 2 oblong loaves or 1 large round loaf.

Sourdough Buttermilk Pancakes

1 ½ cups sourdough starter
2 eggs (separated)
1 cup luke warm buttermilk
2 Tbsp. melted butter
1 cup whole wheat pastry flour
2 Tbsp. sugar
1 ½ tsp. salt
1 tsp. soda

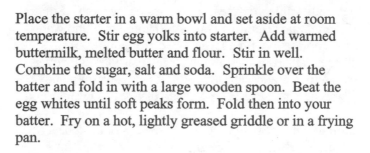

Place the starter in a warm bowl and set aside at room temperature. Stir egg yolks into starter. Add warmed buttermilk, melted butter and flour. Stir in well. Combine the sugar, salt and soda. Sprinkle over the batter and fold in with a large wooden spoon. Beat the egg whites until soft peaks form. Fold then into your batter. Fry on a hot, lightly greased griddle or in a frying pan.

These pancakes are wonderfully light and delicious. Everyone always wants seconds.

Serve them with your favorite syrup or try fresh fruit and whipped cream for a real Sunday morning treat.

This recipe serves 2 to 3 and may be doubled if needed.

From a dear friend

Sourdough Carrot Cake

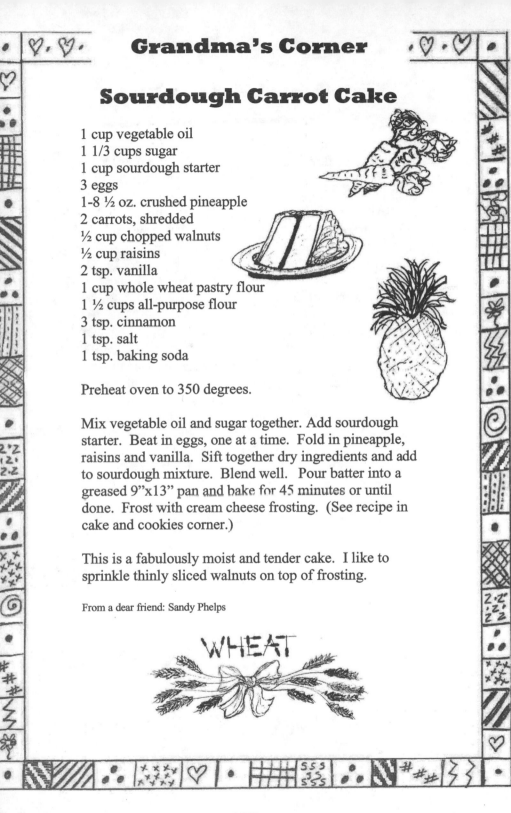

1 cup vegetable oil
1 1/3 cups sugar
1 cup sourdough starter
3 eggs
1-8 ½ oz. crushed pineapple
2 carrots, shredded
½ cup chopped walnuts
½ cup raisins
2 tsp. vanilla
1 cup whole wheat pastry flour
1 ½ cups all-purpose flour
3 tsp. cinnamon
1 tsp. salt
1 tsp. baking soda

Preheat oven to 350 degrees.

Mix vegetable oil and sugar together. Add sourdough starter. Beat in eggs, one at a time. Fold in pineapple, raisins and vanilla. Sift together dry ingredients and add to sourdough mixture. Blend well. Pour batter into a greased 9"x13" pan and bake for 45 minutes or until done. Frost with cream cheese frosting. (See recipe in cake and cookies corner.)

This is a fabulously moist and tender cake. I like to sprinkle thinly sliced walnuts on top of frosting.

From a dear friend: Sandy Phelps

WHEAT

Sourdough Chocolate Cake

2/3 cup butter-flavored
Shortening
1 tsp. salt
1 ½ tsp. baking soda
1 cup sourdough starter
¾ cup cocoa
1 cup chopped walnuts
Or pecans
1¼-cup all-purpose flour

½ tsp. baking powder
1 2/3 cups sugar
3 eggs
1-½ tsp. vanilla
¾ cup whole-wheat
pastry flour
¾ cup water

Preheat oven to 375 degrees.

Cream together shortening and sugar on low speed with electric mixer. Blend in sourdough starter. Combine flour, cocoa, baking powder, salt and soda together. Add to creamed mixture, alternately with water. Mix at low speed until thoroughly blended. Stir in nuts and vanilla. Pour into 2 greased and floured 9" cake pans. Bake for 35 minutes or until toothpick comes out clean when inserted into center of cake.

Allow to cool in pans for 10 minutes. Invert on a wire rack and remove pans carefully.

See frosting section in cakes & cookies corner <u>or</u> use your favorite vanilla or chocolate frosting recipe.

Sourdough English Muffins

1-cup starter (room temperature)
¾ cup buttermilk (room temperature)
1 ½ cups all-purpose flour
1-cup whole-wheat flour
¼ cup yellow cornmeal
½ tsp. salt
1 tsp. soda

Combine all ingredients and mix well with a large wooden spoon. Turn dough onto a lightly floured surface and knead until smooth, you may add more flour if needed. Roll dough out to ½ inch thick. Let rest for 10 minutes. Cut with a floured 3" biscuit cutter or kitchen glass. Sprinkle 2 Tbsp. cornmeal onto a cookie sheet and lightly press each side of muffin into cornmeal to coat them. Cover muffins with plastic wrap and let rise for 1 hour. Fry on a lightly greased griddle at 350 degrees, for 20 minutes. Turn muffins often to ensure a light brown color on both sides.

Store muffins in refrigerator.

These are great toasted with jam or topped with scrambled, over-easy, or poached eggs.

From a dear friend.

Sourdough French Bread

1 ½ cups warm water
1 pkg. active dry yeast
1 cup sourdough starter
2 cups whole wheat flour
6 cups all-purpose flour
2 ½ tsp. sugar
2 tsp. salt
½ tsp. soda

In a large mixing bowl, sprinkle yeast into warm water and stir gently. Add sourdough start, 2 cups whole wheat flour, 2 cups all-purpose flour and sugar to yeast mixture and stir vigorously for 4 minutes. Cover your bowl with a damp cloth and let dough rise in a warm place for 2 hours. Combine salt and soda with 1 cup of remaining flour and mix into dough. Turn dough onto 1 cup of flour spread on a breadboard or counter top. Knead in the flour until well incorporated and the dough is smooth and elastic. More flour may be needed. Shape into 1 large round or 2 oblong loaves. Place on a greased baking sheet, cover and let rise until doubled in size. (About 2 hours)
Preheat oven to 450 degrees. Just before baking, brush the loaves very lightly with vegetable oil and score the tops diagonally 3 to 4 times with a sharp knife. Bake for 35 to 40 minutes. If you prefer a tougher crust, wipe the loaves with salt water 10 minutes before baking is finished.

Fantastic served hot out of the oven with herbed butter with your evening meal. If you have any left in the morning, make French toast for breakfast. A real treat!

Sourdough Fruitcake

2/3 cups vegetable oil
2 ¼ cups sugar
2 eggs
2 cups whole-wheat pastry flour
1 tsp. baking powder
1 tsp. salt
1 ½ tsp. cinnamon
¼ tsp. allspice
¼ tsp. nutmeg
2 cups sourdough starter

½ cup chopped dates
¾ cup snipped, mixed dried fruits
½ cup raisins
½ cup candied red or green cherries
1 cup chopped pecans
½ cup boiling water
1 tsp. baking soda

Preheat oven to 275 degrees.

Cream oil and sugar together until smooth. Add eggs and beat well. Sift flour, baking powder, salt and spices together and add to egg mixture, stirring until well mixed. Stir in sourdough starter. Fold in fruits and nuts. Dissolve the soda in the boiling water and cool to lukewarm. Add to batter and stir just enough to blend in well. Pour into 2 well-greased bread pans and bake for 2 hours or until the cake shrinks from the sides of the pan. Let cool for 10 minutes, remove from pans and place on wire rack to finish cooling.

This delightful fruitcake is always well received. It makes a nice holiday gift.

Makes 2 loaves.

From a dear friend: Ruth Nelson

Sourdough Pancakes

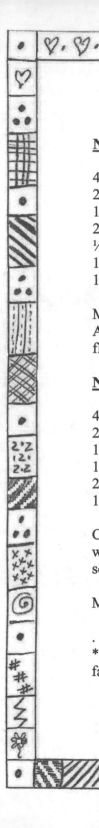

Number 1

4 cups sourdough starter
2 Tbsp. sugar
1 egg
2 Tbsp. melted butter
¼ cup evaporated milk
1 tsp. salt
1 tsp. soda

Mix the starter, egg, melted butter and milk. Beat well. Add remaining ingredients and mix well. Thicken with flour if needed. Fry on a lightly greased griddle. *

Number 2

4 cups sourdough starter
2 eggs
1 tsp. salt
1 Tbsp. sugar
2 Tbsp. vegetable oil
1 tsp. soda

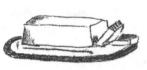

Combine sourdough starter, eggs, salt and sugar and beat well. Add oil and mix again. Just before frying add soda. Fry pancakes on hot, greased griddle. *

Make 3-4 servings.

.

* You may use a vegetable cooking spray, or my favorite is real butter, to fry your pancakes.

Sourdough Pumpkin Roll

3 eggs
1 cup sugar
¾ cup canned pumpkin
1 tsp. lemon juice
½ cup sourdough starter
1 cup whole wheat pastry flour
2 tsp. pumpkin spice
1 tsp. baking powder
¼ tsp. salt
¼ cup powdered sugar
½ cup finely chopped walnuts

Beat eggs and sugar together until thick and lemony color. Stir in pumpkin, lemon juice and sourdough starter. Combine flour, pumpkin spice, baking powder and salt with a wire whisk. Fold into sourdough mixture until blended. Spread onto a greased 15x10x1 inch-baking sheet. Bake for 12 to 15 minutes.

Dust a cotton dishtowel with powdered sugar and sprinkle with the nuts. Invert cake on prepared towel; roll up cake with towel and place on a wire rack to cool. Unroll and spread with cream cheese filling. Roll up and refrigerate for 2 to 3 hours before slicing.

Cream cheese filling:

6 oz. cream cheese
4 Tbsp. butter
1 tsp. vanilla
1 cup powdered sugar

Beat together until smooth.

Serves 10 to 12.

173

Sourdough Spicy Applesauce Cake

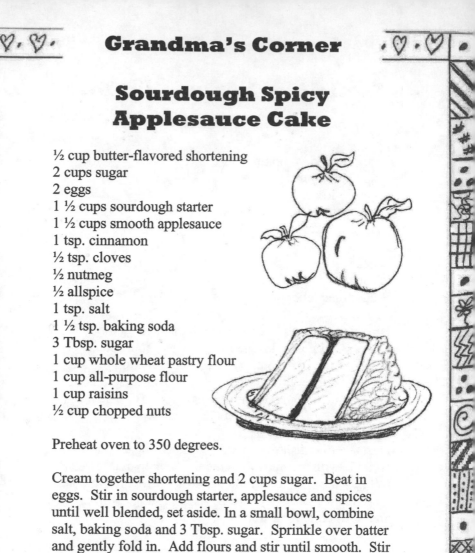

½ cup butter-flavored shortening
2 cups sugar
2 eggs
1 ½ cups sourdough starter
1 ½ cups smooth applesauce
1 tsp. cinnamon
½ tsp. cloves
½ nutmeg
½ allspice
1 tsp. salt
1 ½ tsp. baking soda
3 Tbsp. sugar
1 cup whole wheat pastry flour
1 cup all-purpose flour
1 cup raisins
½ cup chopped nuts

Preheat oven to 350 degrees.

Cream together shortening and 2 cups sugar. Beat in eggs. Stir in sourdough starter, applesauce and spices until well blended, set aside. In a small bowl, combine salt, baking soda and 3 Tbsp. sugar. Sprinkle over batter and gently fold in. Add flours and stir until smooth. Stir in raisins and nuts. Pour into 2 prepared 9" round cake pans. Bake for 25 to 30 minutes or until a toothpick inserted in center of cake comes out clean. Cool in pan 10 minutes then remove to wire racks to cool completely before frosting.

Frost with butter cream frosting. (See cake and cookies corner for recipe.) For a maple frosting you may omit vanilla from this recipe and add maple flavoring in it's place.

Grandma's Corner

Sourdough Starters

Number 1

1 Tbsp. active dry yeast
½ cup warm water
2 tsp. honey
2 ½ cups whole wheat flour
2 cups warm water

Sprinkle yeast into ½ cup warm water. Stir in honey and then gradually add the flour and remaining water. Place mixture into a gallon glass jar or crock. Do not use a metal container because the starter will react chemically with the metal. Cover container with a damp cloth secured with elastic. Keep at room temperature for five days. Stir mixture down every morning with a wooden or plastic spoon. (No metal) Add ¼ cup each of warm water and whole wheat flour on day five. Keep at room temperature for 1 more day, then refrigerate the mixture in a small crock or glass jar.

When you use 1 cup of starter, always replace it with 1 cup each of warm water and whole wheat flour. You must use or discard 1 cup weekly and replace as above to keep your starter fresh.

Number 2

2 ½ cups milk
2 ½ cup flour
½ yeast cake
1 tsp. sugar

Let set for 2 days in a warm place to work. Use required amount in your favorite recipe. Save 1 cup in a pint jar with a tight lid. Refrigerate.

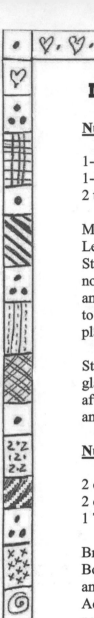

Grandma's Corner

More Sour Dough Starters

Number 3

1-cup whole-wheat flour
1-cup all-purpose flour
2 tsp. Honey

Mix all ingredients together well in a glass jar or crock. Leave uncovered for 4 days in a warm place to ferment. Stir mixture several times a day to aerate. The starter is now ready to use in your favorite recipe. Replace the amount used by adding equal amounts of water and flour to remaining starter. Let stand for 24 hours in a warm place to be ready to use again.

Store unused portion in refrigerator, tightly covered in a glass jar or crock. Shake it daily. To activate it again after storage, add 3 Tbsp. water and 3 Tbsp. flour, stir and store.

Number 4

2 cups luke-warm potato water
2 cups whole-wheat flour
1 Tbsp. honey or sugar

Bring 3 cups of water and 2 potatoes (cut up) to a boil. Boil until the potatoes are tender. Remove the potatoes and measure 2 cups of liquid into a glass jar or crock. Add flour and sugar to water and mix until smooth and pasty. Set in warm place for several days or until doubled in size. Use what you need, then replace with equal amounts of flour and water. Stir and let stand over night at room temperature. Refrigerate in tightly covered jar or crock.

176

Super Peanut Butter Brownies

½ cup butter-flavored shortening
2-1 oz. squares unsweetened chocolate
1 cup sugar
1/3 cup peanut butter
1 egg
½ cup sourdough starter
1 tsp. vanilla
½ cup whole wheat pastry flour
½ tsp. baking soda

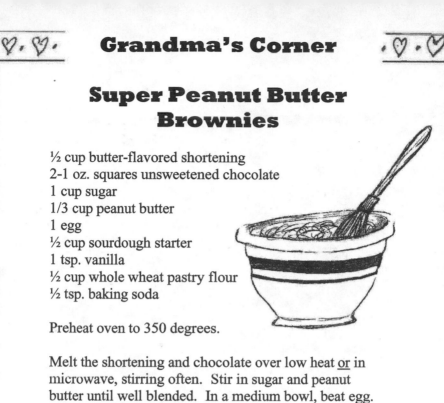

Preheat oven to 350 degrees.

Melt the shortening and chocolate over low heat or in microwave, stirring often. Stir in sugar and peanut butter until well blended. In a medium bowl, beat egg. Then add sourdough starter, vanilla and chocolate mixture and stir well. Set aside. Combine flour and soda and stir into sourdough mixture. Spread into a greased 9"x 9" pan and bake for 25 to 30 minutes or until edges begin to pull away from pan. Cool and frost with cocoa peanut butter frosting. (See cakes and cookies corner.)

You may sprinkle ½ cup chopped peanuts on frosted brownies if desired.

Makes 16 to 18 servings.

From a dear friend.

Kiddies Corner

Blender Animal Crackers

Grind ½ cup oatmeal in blender until fine.
Add the following:
2 tsp. honey (Clover or orange)
½ tsp. salt
¾ cup whole-wheat flour
¼ tsp. baking soda
¼ cup butter or margarine
4 Tbsp. buttermilk

Add into blender ¼ cup butter, 4 Tbsp. buttermilk and blend until dough is formed.
Place dough on a flour surface and roll very thin. Cut with your favorite animal cookie cutters. Place on sprayed cookie sheets and bake at 400 degrees for 10 to 12 minutes.

Your kids are sure to love these yummy crackers!

Doggie Treats to Drool For

No. 1

Preheat oven to 325 degrees

1 cup whole wheat flour
½ cup all purpose flour
¾ cup nonfat dry milk
½ cup quick oats
¼ cup yellow cornmeal

1Tbsp. sugar
1/3 cup margarine
1 egg slightly beaten
1 Tbsp. beef or chicken dissolved in ½ cup hot water.

Mix first 6 ingredients in medium bowl, cut in the margarine forming course crumbs. Mix in egg and slowly add broth stirring with fork until well blended. Turn onto floured board and knead for 5 minutes. Roll out to ½ inch thick and cut into bone shapes. Bake for 30 minutes or until firm and dry to the touch.

No. 2

1 ½ cup whole-wheat flour
1 cup all purpose flour
½ cup dry milk
½ tsp. garlic powder
6 Tbsp. bacon fat
1 egg mixed with ½ cup water

Combine dry ingredients. Mix in bacon fat until cornmeal consistency. Add egg and water, mixing until dough forms. Turn onto floured surface and knead well, adding more flour if dough is too sticky. Roll out and cut into shapes. Place on foil-lined pan and bake for 30 minutes at 325 degrees. Bones should be hard when cooled, if not, bake for 15 to 20 minutes longer.

Fantastic Whole Wheat Pretzels

1 pkg. dry yeast
3 cups whole-wheat flour
1 cup all purpose flour
¼ cup wheat germ
Salt to taste
5 tsp. dark brown sugar
¾ cup hot water
1 egg, slightly beaten
Sesame seeds

Preheat oven to 425 degrees.
Place first 6 ingredients into large mixing bowl. Add the hot water and mix until the dough forms a ball. Place dough on a lightly floured surface and knead for 5 minutes or until your dough is smooth and elastic. Roll walnut size pieces in your hands to form a 5-inch rope and twist into pretzel shapes. Brush with beaten egg and sprinkle with sesame seeds. Place on greased cookies sheets and bake for 10 to 12 minutes until browned. Makes about 2 dozen. Enjoy!

Homemade Finger Paints

½ cup whole wheat flour
1 Tbsp. glycerin
Food coloring or poster paints
Small screw top jars (baby food jars work great)

In a small saucepan mix flour with ½ cup water to form a paste. Stir in remaining water and cook over low heat until mixture becomes clear, stirring constantly. Allow mixture to cool completely and add glycerin and mix well. If mixture seems too thick, add small amounts of water to desired consistency. Pour into jars and add coloring, mix well.

Dip your typing paper or shelf liner into water and lay on washable surface. Dip hands in water then begin your artwork. Does not crack or peel.

Paper paste Made Easy

1/3 cup whole wheat flour
2 Tbsp. sugar
1 cup water
¼ tsp. oil of cinnamon

Add flour and sugar to sauce pan and gradually add water, stirring quickly to break up any lumps. Stirring constantly, cook until mixture is clear. Remove from heat and blend in oil completely. Pour into baby food jars. Will store for several weeks. Makes approx. 1 cup

Kids Applesauce Dump Cake

Into an ungreased 8x8 pan, dump:

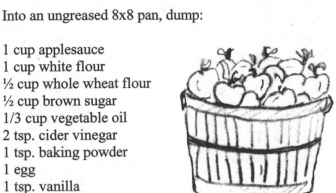

1 cup applesauce
1 cup white flour
½ cup whole wheat flour
½ cup brown sugar
1/3 cup vegetable oil
2 tsp. cider vinegar
1 tsp. baking powder
1 egg
1 tsp. vanilla
½ cup raisins

Stir until well blended. Bake for 20 minutes at 350 degrees.
Serve hot or cold. Great with ice cream.

Popped Wheat Kernels

Simmer whole-wheat kernels until they are plump, tender and begin to split open. Drain and rinse well, removing excess water by rolling in paper towels. In a heavy pan, add enough vegetable or olive oil to deep-fry the wheat kernels and heat to 360 degrees. Add about 1½ cups of the wheat into a wire basket or strainer and pop for 1½ minutes or until popping ceases. Drain on paper towels. Repeat process until all wheat is popped.

Season with any of the following:

Salt, seasoned salt, garlic salt, barbecue spices, onion or celery salt, cinnamon and sugar or any combination you like. These kernels are wonderful on salads, added to your favorite trail mix, or as a topping for ice cream or pudding or just for a quick snack.

Recipes for Man's Best Friend

No.1

1 cup whole-wheat flour
1 cup all purpose flour
½ cup wheat germ
2 tsp. brown sugar
½ cup powdered milk
½ tsp. salt
6 Tbsp. Margarine or vegetable shortening
1 egg
½ cup water

Mix together the flours, wheat germ, dry milk and salt. Cut in shortening. In a small bowl mix egg, sugar and water. Add to dry ingredients to make a stiff dough. Knead on floured surface for 5 minutes. Roll out and cut into desired shapes. Bake at 325 degrees for 20 to 30 minutes or until lightly browned.

No. 2

2 cups whole-wheat flour
¼ cup dry yeast
½ tsp. garlic powder
Beef or chicken broth

Mix together dry ingredients. Slowly add broth to make a stiff dough. Knead for 5 minutes. Quickly roll out and cut into your favorite shapes. Bake at 350 degrees for 15 minutes. Turn off heat and leave the treats in the oven until morning to harden.

Kiddies Corner

Recipe for preserving Children

One or more children, toddlers and up.

Take children and tuck into bed early, Let rest for 12 hours, with door slightly ajar, to admit nightlight coming from the hall. In the morning, dress them and put them in the cheeriest and brightest corner of the kitchen.

To each child serve:

1 cup orange juice
2 slices of homemade whole-wheat toast
1 bowl of Georgie Porgie
1 glass of milk

Remove children to tall green grass; add a brightly colored kite for flying, and a dog or two for chasing. Cover gently with blue sky and play in the sunshine until lightly brown. They are guaranteed to be happily preserved.

Kiddies Corner

Salt Dough Ornaments

1¼-cup water
1 cup salt
1½ cup all purpose flour
½ cup wheat flour

Heat water and salt in pan until salt has dissolved.
Add to flour mixture. Mix with hands until you have s
smooth dough. Roll out and cut with cookie cutters. A
garlic press makes great whiskers for Santa. Place on a
foil-lined cookie sheet. Bake at 300 degrees for about 1
hour. Turn often. You can paint with poster paint or
acrylic paint. Spray with satin varnish for a pretty shine.

Salt Map Mixture

1 cup whole wheat flour
2 cup salt
1 cup water
Poster paints

Mix flour and salt. Add water a little at a time stirring to
combine thoroughly. Divide into bowls and add your
colors. Spread immediately with frosting spreader.
Must be used at once. Will dry solid in 2 to 3 days.

Shredded Wheat & Popcorn Crunch

2 cups bite size shredded wheat biscuits
8 cups popped corn
1 cup toasted slivered almonds
1 cup dark corn syrup
½ cup real butter
1 ½ tsp. vanilla
1 tsp. cinnamon
1 ½ cups sugar

Yummy

Preheat oven to 250 degrees. In a large greased ovenproof pot or casserole dish, stir together shredded wheat, popcorn, and almonds. Heat in the oven for 20 minutes. Keep warm. Grease two large cookie sheets and set aside. In a deep saucepan over medium heat add the sugar, corn syrup and butter. Stir constantly until mixtures comes to full boil. Using a pastry brush that has been dipped in hot water and drained, gently brush down the sides of the pan. Insert candy thermometer and cook without stirring to 290 degrees. Remove from heat and immediately add the vanilla and cinnamon, stirring constantly. Slowly pour the hot sugar syrup over the popcorn mixture stirring constantly until coated well. Spread evenly on prepared cookie sheets. Allow to cool completely. Break into pieces and store in covered container.

Kiddies Corner

Teething Rings

1 cup whole wheat flour
2 Tbsp. sifted soy flour
2 Tbsp. dry milk
2 tsp. raw wheat germ
1 beaten egg
3 Tbsp. honey
2 Tbsp. vegetable oil

Preheat oven to 350 degrees. Lightly mix together the
dry ingredients. Make a well in the center, stir in egg,
honey and oil. Blend thoroughly. Form into a ball and
place on a well-floured surface. Knead until smooth.
Divide dough into 18 pieces and shape as desired. Place
on lightly greased cookie sheet and bake for 10 minutes
or until golden. Store in a tightly covered container

Wheat Chips

These delicious chips are similar to potato chips, but made from whole wheat to create a healthy and tasteful treat.

Yummy

Mix together:
1-cup whole-wheat flour
2 cups cold water
Season to taste with one or more of the following:

½ tsp. each onion and garlic salt
1 tsp. kosher or sea salt
3-4 tsp. Parmesan cheese
1 tsp. of any seasoning like taco, barbecue or ranch

Mix together all your ingredients. Pour mixture into Ketchup type bottle and squirt onto a non-stick sprayed cookie sheet in potato chip shapes. Sprinkle with sesame seeds if desired.

Bake at 350 degrees for 10 to 15 minutes or until crisp. Check and turn chips over occasionally to be sure the middle is cooking as fast as the edges.

Special hint: for a crispier chip, the thinner the better.

Main Dish Corner

Main Dish Corner

American Style Pilaf

3 Tbsp. butter or olive oil
1 green pepper, chopped
2 cups rice, uncooked
2-½ tsp. chicken bouillon granules, diluted in 4 cups boiling water
1 medium onion, chopped or 1/8 cup dried onion, reconstituted
2 cups celery, chopped
2 cups whole wheat berries, cooked

In a medium saucepan, melt butter; sauté onions, green pepper and chopped celery, until tender. Add the rest of the ingredients, and bring to a boil. Cover and simmer for 30 minutes.

From a friend:

Main Dish Corner

Asparagus Filling for Crepes

12 fresh or canned asparagus tips
2 Tbsp. butter or margarine
2 tsp. all-purpose flour
2/3 cup half and half
1 tsp. fresh parsley, chopped
1 tsp. fresh chives, chopped
Salt and pepper to taste
1 Tbsp. Parmesan cheese, grated

Keep crepes warm while preparing filling. If asparagus is fresh, cook in boiling salted water until crisp and tender, drain well. If asparagus is canned, drain well. Melt butter in a small saucepan over low heat. Stir in flour and cook 45 seconds. Stir in half and half and cook, stirring frequently, until thick. Stir in parsley, chives, salt & pepper to taste.

Preheat Broiler to 500 degrees. Stir asparagus into sauce. Divide filling between crepes. Roll up and arrange in a single layer in a shallow casserole dish. Sprinkle with Parmesan cheese. Broil until cheese is melted and lightly browned, approximately 2 minutes.

Serves 4

You can have several different variations; like spinach or tomatoes, or corn and cheddar cheese. Use your imagination and your leftovers!

Main Dish Corner

Beef & Peppers over Wheat Berries

4 – 6 cups cooked wheat berries
1 lb. ground round or round steak, slice very thin and cut
in strips
¼ tsp. garlic powder
Salt & pepper
1-cup beef stock or broth
2 Tbsp. soy sauce
2 Tbsp. cornstarch
2 Tbsp. water
1 cup green pepper, sliced thin
1 tsp. fresh ginger, grated

Brown meat. Add garlic powder, salt and pepper. Add
soup stock to meat. Combine soy sauce, cornstarch and
water in bowl. Add to meat mixture just before it comes
to a boil. Add green pepper and ginger. Cook for just a
minute; peppers should still be crisp.
Serve over hot wheat berries.

Serves 6

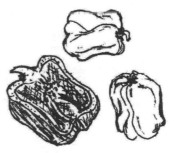

Main Dish Corner

Boston Baked Wheat

4 cups cooked wheat berries
1-cup ketchup
1 onion, chopped, sautéed
1-cup water
½ cup mild molasses
¾ tsp. prepared mustard
3 slices bacon, cut up and fried
Salt/pepper

Combine in casserole dish. Bake 30 minutes at 350 degrees.

From a friend: Jerry Brown

Boston Baked Whole Wheat

4 cups whole kernel wheat
10 cups water
1 lb. bacon cut in fourths
1 large onion, diced
½ tsp. dry mustard

¼ cup molasses
1/3 tsp. pepper
1/3 cup ketchup
2 tsp. salt

In a large roaster or Dutch oven, combine wheat, water, bacon, and onion. Combine remaining ingredients in bowl and pour into pan with wheat. Cover and bake for 6 hours at 200 degrees. Remove. Add a little boiling water if mixture becomes a little dry. Makes 14 cups This casserole freezes well.

From a friend: Sandy Phelps

WHEAT, OUR POT OF AMERICAN GOLD!

Main Dish Corner

Broccoli Wheat Casserole

4 – 5 Tbsp. whole-wheat flour
½ cup cracked wheat - cooked
½ cup butter
2 cups milk
1 medium onion - minced
½ cup grated parmesan cheese
1 egg – beaten
½ tsp. salt & pepper to taste
1 pkg. frozen chopped broccoli or fresh broccoli,
chopped into small bites, cooked
½ cup dry breadcrumbs
1 cup mild cheddar cheese – shredded (optional)

Cook onion in the butter until tender. Add whole-wheat flour and stir in milk gradually. Cook slowly until it thickens, stirring constantly. Add the cooked cracked wheat, parmesan cheese, egg, salt and pepper.
Line the bottom of a casserole dish with the broccoli and pour the sauce over it. Top with breadcrumbs and dab the top with butter and cheddar cheese (optional). Bake at 350 degrees for 30 – 35 minutes.

Serves 6

Main Dish Corner

Cabbage Rolls

12 large cabbage leaves
¼ lb. ground pork <u>or</u> sausage
1 lb. ground beef
2 tsp. salt and pepper to taste
1 cup uncooked cracked wheat
1 onion, minced
2-8 oz. cans tomato sauce
¼ cup brown sugar
¼ cup vinegar

Crack wheat. Place cabbage leaves in a large bowl.
Cover with boiling water and let sit until leaves are
wilted, drain thoroughly. (Leaves should roll easily
without splitting.) Combine meats, salt, pepper, cracked
wheat, onion and 1 can of the tomato sauce. Place a
small portion of meat mixture on center of each cabbage
leaf. Fold ends over and roll up. Place a toothpick over
the seam to hold the cabbage in place and put seam side
down in skillet. Combine the rest of the ingredients and
pour over the cabbage rolls. Simmer covered for 1 hour;
baste often.

Serves 6

Main Dish Corner

Cheesy Tomato Bake

3 cups cooked whole-wheat berries
6 slices bacon
4 Tbsp. flour
3 cups tomato juice
1 tsp salt
¼ cup onion, diced
1 cup grated cheese (cheddar or American)
Breadcrumbs (optional)

Dice bacon and fry. Add flour, tomato juice and onion
to make sauce. Remove from fire and add grated cheese.
Pour over wheat and place in buttered baking dish. Top
with more cheese and breadcrumbs, if desired. Bake at
350 degrees for 45 minutes.

Grandma's days....

WHEAT,
OUR POT OF
AMERICAN
GOLD !

Main Dish Corner

Chicken Bake

1-cup cooked wheat berries
1/3-cup onion, chopped
2 Tbsp. butter <u>or</u> margarine
1 ½ cup cooked, diced chicken
1 can cream of chicken soup
1-cup milk
1 cup mild cheddar cheese, grated
1 cup buttered breadcrumbs

WHEAT, OUR POT OF AMERICAN GOLD !

Sauté onions in butter. Stir in the rest of the ingredients except for ¼ cup cheese and breadcrumbs. Spread out in a 9" x 9" baking dish and sprinkle cheese and breadcrumbs on top. Bake at 350 degrees for 30 minutes.

From a friend: Sandy Phelps

MILK

202

Main Dish Corner

Chili-Cheese Bake

1 cup cracked wheat
3 medium zucchini, sliced
1 7-½ oz. can green chilies, diced
¾ lb. Monterey jack cheese, shredded
1 large tomato, thinly sliced
Salt
1 pt. Sour cream
1 tsp. garlic salt
1 tsp. oregano
2 Tbsp. chopped green peppers
2 Tbsp. chopped onion
2 Tbsp. parsley, minced

Cook cracked wheat in 3 cups water and ½ tsp. salt.
Cook zucchini in ¼ cup salted water until slightly
tender. Butter a 3 qt. casserole dish and spread cooked
wheat on bottom of dish. Cover with chopped chilies.
Sprinkle ½ the cheese on top. Arrange the zucchini
slices on top of cheese. Cover with tomato slices, and
sprinkle with salt. Combine the sour cream, garlic salt,
oregano, bell pepper and onion. Spread over tomato
layer. Sprinkle remaining cheese on top. Bake at 350
degrees for 45 min. or until heated through. Sprinkle
parsley on top and serve immediately.

Serves 6

From a friend: Sandy Phelps

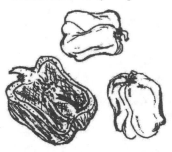

Chili Relleno

1 large can whole Ortega green chilies (6)
1 ½ cup evaporated milk
4 eggs
3 Tbsp. whole-wheat flour
1 lb. cheddar cheese, shredded
1 lb. Monterey jack cheese, shredded
1 8 oz. can tomato sauce
1 lb. ground beef, browned, drained
1 can black olives, chopped
1 medium onion, chopped

Split chilies, spread on bottom of 9"x 13" baking dish.
Add cooked ground beef, black olives & onions.
Combine milk, eggs, and whole-wheat flour in bowl.
Blend. Pour over chilies. Add a layer of cheddar cheese
(use all the cheddar cheese). Bake 30 minutes at 325
degrees. Top with tomato sauce then Monterey Jack
cheese. Bake an additional 15 minutes or until bubbly.

Serves 8

From a friend:

WHEAT,
OUR POT OF
AMERICAN
GOLD !

Main Dish Corner

Chinese Fried Wheat

3 cups cooked cold wheat berries
¼ lb. finely diced ham or bacon
¼ cup cooking oil
4 green onions sliced <u>or</u> 1 medium onion minced
¾ tsp. salt
2 Tbsp. soy sauce
2 eggs

Place meat in hot heavy skillet and stir-fry about 5 minutes until browned and cooked thoroughly. Add oil, wheat, green onions, salt and soy sauce. Cook and stir until heated through. Hollow a center in the wheat and break in eggs. Scramble until eggs are cooked; then stir into the balance of the mixture.

Serves 6

From a friend: Sandy Phelps

Italian Fried Wheat

3 cups cooked wheat berries   1 tsp. garlic powder
¼ cup cooking oil   <u>or</u> salt
Italian seasoning to taste   Leftover hamburgers,
¾ tsp salt   roast, etc.
1 16 oz. can diced tomatoes   Parmesan Cheese

Prepare wheat the same as for Chinese fried wheat. Heat oil in skillet then add wheat, Italian seasonings, meat and tomatoes.
Sprinkle with Parmesan cheese.

Chow Mein

1 lb. pork strips, cut in bite-size pieces
4 Tbsp. shortening or olive oil
1-cup water
1 green pepper, sliced
2 onions, sliced
4 cups celery, sliced
2 cups bean sprouts
2 carrots, julienne style
1 pkg. frozen snow pea pods
1- 4 oz. can mushrooms, drained
¼ cup soy sauce
3 Tbsp. cornstarch in ½ cup water
1-cup wheat sprouts

Sauté` pork strips in shortening until browned. Remove meat. Add water, green pepper, onions, mushrooms, and celery, simmer for 10 minutes. Add bean sprouts, carrots, and pea pods, cook 5 minutes more. Add soy sauce and cornstarch-water mixture and cook until thickened. Remove from heat and add wheat sprouts, tossing lightly.
Serve over chow mein noodles.

Serves 8

From a friend:

**WHEAT,
OUR POT OF
AMERICAN
GOLD !**

Main Dish Corner

Corned Beef N Biscuits

2 Tbsp. butter
1 medium onion, chopped
2 ½ cup fresh tomatoes or 1 qt. jar canned tomatoes
½ cup cracked wheat
1 can corned beef
Biscuits for topping (see biscuit section or use
refrigerator biscuits and cut each piece into 4 sections)

Crack ½ cup wheat. Sauté onion in the butter. Add
tomatoes, cracked wheat, and corned beef. Stir until
well blended. Bring to a boil, stirring constantly. Let
simmer about 15 minutes until thick and smooth. Pour
into ungreased 2 qt. baking dish. Put biscuits on top and
bake at 350 degrees for 30 – 35 minutes or until biscuits
are browned.

Serves 4

Corned Beef Casserole

1 can cream of mushroom soup
1-cup milk
1- 4 oz. can mushrooms, drained
2 cups cooked cracked wheat
1 can corned beef
1 cup grated mild cheddar cheese
½ cup celery, chopped (optional)

Combine all ingredients above in a 1-½ qt. casserole
dish. Bake at 350 degrees for 30 minutes.
Garnish with a side of coleslaw.

A Favorite !

WHEAT,
OUR POT OF
AMERICAN
GOLD !

Main Dish Corner

Cracked Wheat Casserole

1 lb. Ground beef
½ cup chopped onion (1 medium)
1 small garlic clove, minced
1 ½ cups water
½ cup uncooked cracked wheat
2 Tbsp. chopped parsley
1 tsp. beef bouillon (or 2 cubes)
½ tsp. salt
¼ tsp. oregano leaves
¼ tsp pepper
¼ cup Parmesan cheese
1 cup chopped tomato (fresh or canned)

WHEAT, OUR POT OF AMERICAN GOLD !

Brown ground beef with onion and garlic. Drain.
Combine with the rest of ingredients except the cheese
and tomato.

Bake in tightly covered 1 ½ quart casserole dish for 45
minutes or until the cracked wheat is tender and water
has been absorbed. Stir in cheese and tomato.
Let stand 5 minutes before serving.

Makes 6 servings

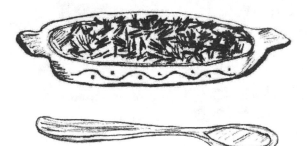

Main Dish Corner

Cracked Wheat Meat Loaf

1 ¼ cup cooked cracked wheat (or bulgar wheat)
1 egg
½ tsp. salt
¾ tsp. sage
¼ tsp. chopped onion
1/8 tsp. pepper
2 tsp. Worcestershire sauce
½ cup ketchup
1 lb. ground beef

Blend ingredients together. Turn into loaf pan or shape
into loaf in a shallow baking pan. If desired, spread
surface with thin layer of ketchup or barbeque sauce.
Bake at 325 degrees or 350 degrees for 1 hour or until
nicely browned.
This meatloaf freezes well.

Serves 6 – 8

From a friend: Jeri Brown

WHEAT,
OUR POT OF
AMERICAN
GOLD !

Main Dish Corner

Franks N Wheat

6 franks (hot dogs)
2 cups cooked wheat berries
1 cup diced apples
¼ cup diced onion (optional)
1 can tomato soup

In a quart casserole dish, combine wheat, apple and
onion. Pour tomato soup over and mix well. Cut franks
in chunks and stir into the above. Cover with aluminum
foil and bake at 400 degrees for 20 – 30 minutes.
Uncover and bake 10 more minutes.

Serves 4

From a friend:

Main Dish Corner

Fried Whole Wheat

2 – 3 Tbsp. cooking oil (olive oil is preferred)
1 cup coarsely chopped onion (1 medium onion)
1 cup green pepper
1 cup shredded carrots
2 cup leftover meat (bacon, ham, chicken, shrimp)
2 cup cooked wheat berries
¼ cup soy sauce
½ tsp salt/ pepper to taste
2 eggs

In a large skillet, sauté onion, green peppers and carrots
in oil. Add meat and whole wheat. Add 2 slightly
beaten eggs, soy sauce and salt. Stir until
cooked.

Serves 6

From a friend:

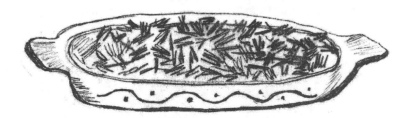

211

Main Dish Corner

Hamburger Casserole

1 lb. lean ground beef
¼ cup onion, chopped
¼ cup green pepper, chopped
½ cup mixed vegetables, chopped (you can use corn)
1 tsp. salt
¼ tsp. ground cumin
¼ tsp. ground marjoram
¼ tsp. black pepper
1 tsp. poultry seasoning
1 cup uncooked cracked wheat or 1 cup bulgur
2 cups boiling water
1-cup tomato juice
1 8 oz. can tomato sauce

In a large skillet, brown ground beef with onions, peppers, veggies and all spices. Simmer over medium heat 5 minutes. Preheat over to 325 degrees. In a 3 qt. casserole dish, combine meat mixture, cracked wheat or bulgur, 2 cups boiling water, tomato juice and tomato sauce. Bake uncovered about 1-½ hours until cracked wheat or bulgur is tender. If casserole has absorbed most of the liquid after 1 hour, cover for the final 30 minutes.

Serve 6

Main Dish Corner

Kibbi

1 ½ cup fine bulgar (crushed wheat)
2 lbs. lean ground beef
¼ tsp. ground allspice
Pinch of ground nutmeg
Pinch of cinnamon
3 tsp. salt
Freshly ground black pepper
1 large onion – finely chopped
Stuffing:
2 Tbsp. pine nuts
1 medium onion – chopped
¼ lb. ground beef (lean)
½ tsp. salt – freshly ground black pepper
Pinch of allspice

Place the bulgar in a bowl; pour in enough warm
water to cover it by several inches. Let it soak for
about 30 minutes or until it doubles in size. Drain
wheat and squeeze excess water out with your
hands. Drop the bulgar into a deep mixing bowl,
add ground beef, (moisten your hands from time to
time with cold water.) Knead until the mixture is
smooth. Knead in the spices, onions, salt, and a few
grindings of pepper. Pat ½ the mixture into a 11 x 9
inch pan. Set the other half of mixture aside while
you prepare the stuffing. Sauté in a large skillet the
¼ lb. beef and onions until lightly browned. Add
pine nuts and spices, spread this stuffing on the
mixture in the pan and then press remaining wheat
and beef mixture evenly on top of stuffing. Score
in diamond shapes and dot with butter. Bake for
about 45 minutes or until brown. Drain off any fat.

From a friend: Sandy Phelps

WHEAT

Main Dish Corner

Lasagna

1 Tbsp. olive oil
1 medium onion, chopped
1 clove garlic, minced
1 lb. ground beef
½ tsp. salt
1- 8 oz. can tomato sauce
1- 14.5 oz can diced tomatoes <u>or</u> 2 cups fresh chopped tomatoes
2 tsp. honey <u>or</u> ¼ cup ketchup
1 bay leaf
½ cup uncooked cracked wheat
½ lb. mozzarella cheese
1 pkg. lasagna noodles <u>or</u> see section for homemade noodles
½ tsp. oregano
1-pint cottage cheese
Parmesan cheese

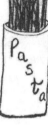

Crack ½ cup wheat. Cook onion and garlic in oil until transparent. Add meat, cook and stir until browned. Add salt, tomatoes, tomato sauce, honey and oregano. Add the bay leaf on top and cover and simmer 45 minutes, stirring occasionally. Add cracked wheat the last 20 minutes. Add a little water if it seems too thick. Shred mozzarella cheese. Cook the noodles following the package directions. Drain, rinse with cold water. Pour a little sauce in a 2 qt. casserole dish; top with 1/3 of the noodles and 1/3 of the cottage cheese and mozzarella cheese. Sprinkle with Parmesan cheese, cover with sauce. Repeat process until ingredients are used. Bake at 350 degrees for 45 minutes.

Serves 6

WHEAT, OUR POT OF AMERICAN GOLD !

Main Dish Corner

Mexican Casserole

1 ½ cup cracked wheat
1 cup freshly chopped tomatoes or 1 14.5 oz. can diced tomatoes
2 ½ cup water
1-4 oz. can diced green chilies
1 Tbsp. Knorr chicken bouillon granules
1 cup onion, chopped
1 tsp. salt – pepper to taste
1 tsp garlic salt
1 8oz. can tomato sauce w/water to clean out can
4 strips of crisp bacon, crumbled or ½ cup Bac -o-bits
Grated cheddar cheese
1 can black olives (optional)

Crack 1½ cups wheat. Combine all ingredients except bacon in a 9" x 9" baking dish. Sprinlke bacon pieces on top. Bake at 350 degrees for one hour. Add a layer of grated cheese over the top 15 min. before casserole is done.
Garnish with black olives

Serves 6

Main Dish Corner

Microwave Fancy Baked Chicken

2 cup boiling water
1-cup bulgur wheat
1 tsp. instant chicken bouillon granules <u>or</u> cubes
1/8 tsp. pepper
2 Tbsp. butter <u>or</u> margarine
¼ cup seasoned breadcrumbs
2 Tbsp. Parmesan cheese
¼ tsp garlic powder
1/8 tsp. paprika
2 whole medium chicken breasts (about 1 ½ lbs.)
skinned, boned and halved lengthwise

In a large microwave safe casserole dish, combine water, bulgur, bouillon granules and pepper. Cook in microwave oven, covered, on 100 percent power (high) for 4 to 5 minutes or until bulgur is done, stirring once. In a glass-measuring cup melt butter. Combine breadcrumbs, cheese, garlic powder and paprika. Brush meaty side of each piece of chicken with some of the melted butter. Coat same side with crumb mixture. Place chicken crumb side up, on microwave safe rack in microwave safe dish. Cook on high 6 – 7 minutes until chicken is tender.

Serve with bulgur mixture.

From a friend: Sandy Phelps

WHEAT, OUR POT OF AMERICAN GOLD !

Main Dish Corner

Mozzarella/Crouton Filling for Crepes

¼ cup butter <u>or</u> margarine
1 (1-inch) thick sliced bread, cubed
1 cup Mozzarella cheese, shredded
Salt and pepper to taste
1/3 cup Parmesan cheese, grated

Heat butter in a small skillet over medium heat. Add bread cubes and cook, stirring often, until golden brown. Remove from heat and stir in Mozzarella cheese. Season with salt and pepper.

Preheat broiler to approximately 500 degrees, divide filling between 4 crepes. Roll up and arrange in a single layer in a shallow heatproof casserole dish. Sprinkle Parmesan cheese on top. Broil until lightly browned, about 2 minutes.

Main Dish Corner

Mushroom Filling for Crepes

¼ cup butter <u>or</u> margarine
1 cup mushrooms, thinly sliced
½ cup all-purpose flour
1 ¼ cups milk
¼ tsp. grated nutmeg
Salt and pepper to taste
1 Tbsp. parsley, chopped
1 Tbsp. Parmesan cheese (optional)

Keep crepes warm while preparing filling. Melt butter in a saucepan over low heat. Add the mushrooms; cover and cook 5-6 minutes. Stir in flour and cook 1 minute. Gradually stir in milk. Bring to a boil, stirring constantly, then simmer for a few additional minutes. Season with nutmeg, parsley and salt/pepper to taste.

Preheat oven to 350 degrees. Divide filling between crepes. Roll up and arrange in a single layer in a casserole dish. Cover with foil. Bake for 20-25 minutes. Add Parmesan cheese the last 5 minutes while uncovered.

Serves 4

WHEAT, OUR POT OF AMERICAN GOLD !

Main Dish Corner

Mushrooms & Wheat

4 to 6 cups cooked wheat
1 can cream of mushroom soup
½ cup milk
1 medium onion, chopped and sautéed

Mix together all ingredients and bake in a casserole dish
for 20 to 30 minutes, at 350 degrees. For a variety, add
chopped celery and green peppers. Heat and serve.

From a friend: Jerry Brown

Bulgur Pilaf with Veggies

1 cup uncooked bulgur
1 Tbsp. olive oil
¾ cup chopped onion
2 cloves garlic, minced
½ lb. zucchini, thinly sliced

1 14½ oz. can diced
tomatoes
1 cup chicken broth
1 tsp. dried basil leaves
1/8 tsp. pepper

Rinse bulgur thoroughly in colander under cold water,
picking out any debris. Drain well; set aside. Heat oil in
large saucepan over medium heat. Add onion and garlic;
cook and stir 3 minutes or until onion is tender. Stir in
zucchini and tomatoes; reduce heat to medium-low.
Cook covered, 15 minutes, or until zucchini is almost
tender, stirring occasionally.
Stir chicken broth, bulgur, basil and pepper into
vegetable mixture. Bring to boil over high heat. Reduce
heat to low. Cook covered, over low heat 15 minutes or
until bulgur is tender and liquid is almost completely
absorbed. Remove from heat; let stand covered 10
minutes. Stir gently before serving.

Makes 8 servings

Main Dish Corner

Parmesan/Potato Filling
for Crepes

2 Tbsp. olive oil
2 Tbsp. butter <u>or</u> margarine
2 ea. Medium potatoes, boiled and diced into small
pieces
Salt and Pepper to taste
1 cup crushed croutons
¼ cup butter <u>or</u> margarine
1 Tbsp. fresh parsley, chopped
2/3 cup Parmesan cheese, grated

Heat oil and 2 Tbsp. butter in skillet over medium-high
heat. Add potatoes and cook until crisp and golden.
Season with salt and pepper.

Preheat broiler: Spoon potato mixture into center of 4
crepes. Roll up and arrange in a single layer in a
shallow casserole dish. In a small bowl, combine
crushed croutons, melted butter, and chopped parsley;
sprinkle over crepes. Top with Parmesan cheese. Broil
approximately 6 inches from heat until crisp and golden
and for about 4-5 minutes.

Serves 4

Main Dish Corner

Pilaf

¼ cup butter
3 Tbsp. cooking oil (olive)
1 clove garlic, minced
1 carrot, julienne style <u>or</u> shredded (optional)
1 sm. can sliced water chestnuts (optional)
1 Tbsp. green onion, chopped
½ cup onion, chopped
1 cup cracked wheat
1 beef or chicken bouillon
2 ½ cups water <u>or</u> broth
Slivered almonds (optional)

Crack 1 cup wheat. Sauté carrots, garlic, and onion in
butter and oil (do not sauté green onion or chestnuts).
Add cracked wheat, bouillon cube and water. Pour into
a baking dish, add water chestnuts. Bake at 350 degrees
for 45 minutes. Add ½ cup slivered almonds if desired.
Garnish with green onion

Serves 4

From a friend:

WHEAT,
OUR POT OF
AMERICAN
GOLD !

Main Dish Corner

Porcupines

1 lb. ground beef
1 ½ cup cracked wheat, uncooked
1 tsp. salt
Add pepper to taste
¼ cup onion, minced
½ cup water
1 tsp. Worcestershire sauce
1-10-¾ oz. can tomato soup

Mix together wheat, ground beef, onion, salt and pepper.
Form into 8 meatballs. Place meatballs in casserole
dish.
Combine in saucepan, tomato soup, water, and
Worcestershire sauce. Pour over meatballs. Cover and
bake at 350 degrees for approx. 1-½ hours. The tomato
mixture should cover the meatballs completely.

Serves 4

WHEAT,
OUR POT OF
AMERICAN
GOLD !

222

Main Dish Corner

Pork Chops over Wheat

4 pork chops
4 Tbsp. oil (olive)
½ cup celery, sliced
½ cup onion, chopped
1 cup uncooked cracked wheat
2-8oz. cans tomato sauce
1 ½ cup water
1 tsp. salt
½ tsp. basil
2 Tbsp. brown sugar
2 Tbsp. ketchup

In a large skillet, brown 4 pork chops in oil. Remove chops and sauté celery and onion. Add uncooked cracked wheat, tomato sauce, water, salt, basil, brown sugar and ketchup.
Bring to a boil. Simmer, covered for 30 minutes. Stir occasionally. Place the pork chops on top of the simmering mixture the last 10 minutes.

Serves 4

From a friend:

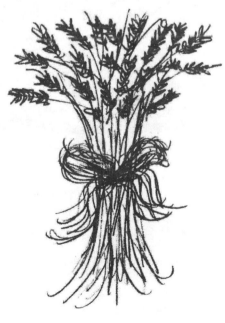

Main Dish Corner

Quiche Lorraine

1 wheat piecrust – see desserts corner
1 cup Swiss cheese, shredded
4 eggs
2 cups half & half cream
1/3 tsp. nutmeg
1/3 tsp. cayenne
1 tsp. sugar
10 slices bacon, fried crispy and crumbled or ½ cup Bac-o-bits

Make your wheat pie crust as given in the dessert corner, cut sugar portion to 1 tsp. Press firmly into a 9" pie plate. Place cheese in a bowl. Add eggs, half and half, nutmeg, cayenne, and sugar. Mix with wire whip only until mixed thoroughly. Sprinkle crumbled bacon in the pie shell and pour filling over it. Bake at 425 degrees for 15 minutes. Lower temp. to 300 degrees for 20 minutes more. A knife inserted into the center of the pie should come out clean when it is done.

Serves 6

Main Dish Corner

Quick Pioneer Stew

2 cans kidney beans – drained (you can also use dried beans, but it takes longer to prepare)
1- 14 ½ oz. can beef broth <u>or</u> cold water
1 tsp. salt
½ to 1 pound beef (browned)
½ cup chopped onion
½ cup finely diced green pepper
1 can (16 oz.) whole kernel corn, undrained
1 can (16 oz.) dices tomatoes, undrained
½ tsp. chili powder
¾ tsp. salt
½ to 1 cup shredded mild cheddar cheese
½ cup cooked wheat berries
1 Tbsp. flour

In skillet cook ground beef, chopped onion, and green pepper until meat is browned. Drain off fat. Add meat mixture to corn, tomatoes, beans and wheat berries. Add chili powder and salt to taste. Simmer 20 minutes. Combine 1 Tbsp. flour with 2 Tbsp. cold water, stir into stew. Cool and stir until thickened and bubbly. Add cheese to the top just before eating.

Serves 8

From a friend:

Main Dish Corner

Salmon Quiche

1 cup whole-wheat flour
1½ cup shredded sharp or mild cheddar cheese
¼ cup chopped or slivered almonds
½ tsp. salt (sea salt)
¼ tsp. paprika
6 Tbsp. cooking oil (can be olive or corn)
1 (15 ½ oz.) can salmon
3 eggs (beaten)
1 cup dairy sour cream
¼ cup mayonnaise or salad dressing
1 Tbsp. grated onion
¼ tsp. dried dill weed
A few drops bottled hot pepper sauce (to your taste)

For crust, combine the whole-wheat flour, ¾ cup of the cheese, the almonds, salt and paprika in a bowl. Stir in the oil. Set aside ½ cup of the crust mixture. Press remaining mixture into the bottom and up the sides of a 9" pie plate. Bake crust in 400 degree oven for 10 minutes. Remove from oven. Reduce oven temperature to 325 degrees.
For filling: Drain salmon, reserve the liquid. Add water to reserved liquid, if necessary, to make ½ cup liquid. Flake salmon, removing any bones or skin. Set aside. In a bowl, blend together eggs, sour cream, mayonnaise or salad dressing and reserved salmon liquid. Stir in salmon, remaining cheese, onion, dill weed and hot pepper sauce. Spoon filling into crust. Sprinkle with reserved crust mixture. Bake in 325 degree oven for 45 minutes or until firm in center.

Makes 6 servings

Main Dish Corner

Sausage & Wheat Casserole

2 ½ cups cooked wheat berries
½ lb. pork sausage
1 medium onion, chopped
½ cup green peppers <u>or</u> ¼ cup dried peppers + ½ cup hot water
1 tsp. seasoned salt
Black pepper to taste
½ tsp. garlic salt
½ tsp. Italian seasoning
1-16 oz. can diced tomatoes
1-cup tomato juice
1-cup mild cheddar cheese

Brown sausage in a large skillet. Add onions and peppers. Cook over medium-low heat until tender. Stir in all the seasonings, tomatoes and tomato juice. Simmer another 5 minutes.
Stir in cooked wheat. Cover and simmer 15 minutes until wheat is hot. Sprinkle top with cheese before serving.

Serves 6

Note: You may also stir in 1 – 2 cups cooked rice for a variation.

Shrimp Jambalaya

2 cups cooked wheat berries
2 Tbsp.butter or margarine
1 Tbsp. all purpose flour
1 clove garlic, minced
1 green pepper, chopped
½ cup onion, chopped
1-cup fresh tomatoes <u>or</u> 1- 14.5 oz. can diced tomatoes,
reserve juice and use in place of water
½ cup water
½ tsp. salt
Pepper to taste
¼ tsp. thyme
2 Tbsp. Worcestershire sauce
1-6 oz. can shrimp <u>or</u> ½ lb.fresh shrimp
1-cup tomato juice
¾ cup pepper jack cheese, grated
2 Tbsp. parsley

Melt butter or margarine in saucepan, add onions, green
peppers and garlic, and cook until tender. Stir in flour
and blend thoroughly. Add tomatoes, water, salt,
pepper, thyme, and Worcestershire sauce, stir
occasionally. Add wheat and shrimp then toss. Sprinkle
parsley over the top and place in a 350-degree oven for
15 minutes.

Serves 6

Main Dish Corner

Sloppy Joes

1 lb. ground beef
1 small onion, chopped
¼ cup green pepper, chopped
1 can tomato soup <u>or</u> tomato sauce thinned w/1 cup
tomato juice
1 tsp. chili powder
1 ½ cooked wheat berries
1 tsp. salt
Pepper to taste

Sauté ground beef, onions and green peppers. Add soup
or sauce/juice, salt and pepper, and cooked wheat. Add
chili powder and simmer for 20-30 minutes until desired
thickness is reached. Serve on buns or over rice.

From a friend: Jeri Brown

WHEAT,
OUR POT OF
AMERICAN
GOLD !

Main Dish Corner

Sloppy Joes from your Stored Goods

½ to 1 cup sprouted wheat – see Sprouted Wheat
Section
¼ cup dried chopped peppers
¼ cup dried chopped onion
2 Tbsp. dried chopped celery
About 1 ¼ cups hot water
1- lb. lean ground beef
1- 8 oz. can tomato paste
1- 8 oz. can tomato sauce
¼ cup ketchup
Dash of hot pepper sauce
¼ tsp. chili powder
1 tsp. cider vinegar
Salt/pepper to taste

WHEAT,
OUR POT OF
AMERICAN
GOLD !

Combine onion, peppers, celery and 1 cup hot water
in a medium bowl. Let stand 10 – 15 minutes to
rehydrate. Add remaining ¼ cup water if needed. In
a large skillet, brown ground beef. Stir in
rehydrated vegetables. Stir over medium low heat
until tender but not browned, 2 minutes. Stir in
remaining ingredients. Cover and simmer 15
minutes. Spoon over hamburger buns.

Makes 4 – 6 servings

Soup
Kettle

Main Dish Corner

Spanish Wheat

3 strips bacon <u>or</u> 2 – 3 tbsp bacon drippings <u>or</u> butter
1 medium onion, chopped
1 green pepper, diced finely
3 cups cooked wheat berries
Salt and pepper to taste
1 tsp. basil (optional)
1 16 oz. can diced tomatoes or 1 qt. jar tomatoes

Brown bacon strips and remove from skillet. In bacon drippings or butter cook onion and green peppers until soft. Add wheat and tomatoes, salt/pepper and basil (optional), cover and simmer in tightly covered pan for several hours. Taste frequently. The longer the wheat cooks, the more it absorbs the flavor. Watch to make sure the liquid has not run dry. Add crumbled bacon before serving.

From a friend: Jeri Brown

Main Dish Corner

Spanish Wheat Dish

4 to 6 cups cooked cracked wheat
1 cup onion, chopped
2 Tbsp. olive oil
1 qt. jar tomatoes, undrained or 2 - 16 oz. cans diced
tomatoes
1 8 oz. can tomato sauce
1 clove garlic, minced
1- 4 oz. can green chilies
1 tsp. garlic powder
1 tsp. chicken flavored granules
1 tsp. salt
¼ cup ketchup
1 ½ cups cheddar cheese, grated
1 can sliced olives (optional)

Put olive oil in a large fry pan and sauté onions, and
garlic until tender. Add tomatoes, tomato sauce,
spices, ketchup and green chilies. Cook 10 minutes
more. Add cooked cracked wheat and continue
cooking for another 10 minutes to heat through.

Serve with cheese on top and garnish with black
olives.

Serves 6 – 8

WHEAT,
OUR POT OF
AMERICAN
GOLD !

Main Dish Corner

Sweet & Sour Wheat Balls

1 ½ cup coarsely cracked wheat
¾ cup dry cracked wheat cooked 5 minutes in ½ cup boiling water
1 cup or more ground beef
2 eggs
¾ tsp. salt
½ tsp. pepper
¼ cup pineapple juice
½ cup onion, minced
1 ½ tsp. beef soup base (or bouillon cubes)

Mix ingredients together. Form into small balls, fry in small amount of oil on medium heat. Add to thickened sweet and sour sauce.

Sauce

Heat   2 Tbsp. oil
        2 cups pineapple juice
Thicken with 3 Tbsp. cornstarch in 2/3 cup water
Add   1 Tbsp. soy sauce
        3 Tbsp. vinegar
        ¾ cup honey or brown sugar
Cook until thick and clear.

Add meatballs and 1 green pepper, chopped, and 1 can pineapple chunks, drained. Heat through, Serve over hot, fluffy rice.

From a friend: Jeri Brown

Main Dish Corner

Tamale Corn Bake

1-cup cornmeal
2 cups water
1 tsp. salt
2 tsp. chili powder
¼ tsp. garlic salt <u>or</u> powder
1 lb. ground beef
1 Tbsp. olive oil <u>or</u> shortening
½ cup chopped onion
¼ cup chopped green pepper
¼ cup uncooked cracked wheat
1 Tbsp. whole-wheat flour
1-14.5 oz can diced tomatoes
1 cup grated mild cheddar cheese

Cook cornmeal, water, and salt in a saucepan until thick. Line bottom of a greased shallow 1-½ qt. casserole dish with the cornmeal mush and set aside.
Brown ground beef, onion, and green pepper in oil in large skillet. Blend in flour, tomatoes, cracked wheat, chili powder, and garlic salt. Simmer 5 minutes. Turn into cornmeal crust. Bake at 350 degrees for 30 minutes. Sprinkle cheese on top – last 10 minutes.

Serves 6

From a friend:

WHEAT, OUR POT OF AMERICAN GOLD !

Main Dish Corner

Tossed Wheat with Ham

2 cups cooked cracked wheat <u>or</u> cooked wheat berries
1/3-cup onion, chopped
1-4 oz. can mushrooms, drained
¼ cup green pepper, chopped
1 clove garlic, minced
2 Tbsp. butter
1 can cream of chicken soup
1-cup fresh tomatoes, chopped <u>or</u> 1-14.5 oz can diced
tomatoes, drained
1 ½ cup diced cooked ham

In a skillet, sauté onion, mushrooms, green pepper, and
garlic in butter until tender. Combine with the rest of the
ingredients in a 1-½ qt. casserole dish. Bake in 350
degrees oven for 30 – 40 minutes.

Serves 6

WHEAT,
OUR POT OF
AMERICAN
GOLD !

Main Dish Corner

Tuna Casserole

2 cups cooked cracked wheat
1 ½ cups water
2-6-½ oz. can tuna
Salt & pepper to taste
1 medium onion, chopped
1 can peas (optional) drained
1 small can mushrooms, drained (optional)
1 can canned evaporated milk or 1½ cup fresh milk
1 ½ cup grated mild cheddar cheese or American cheese
Cornflakes or breadcrumbs for topping
Butter

Mix together cooked cracked wheat, tuna, onion, salt/pepper, mushrooms and peas in a 9" x 9" baking dish. Combine milk and 1 cup cheese together, stir and pour over mixture. Sprinkle remaining cheese and cornflakes or breadcrumbs over the top of casserole. Dot with pats of butter. Bake 30 – 40 minutes at 350 degrees.

From a friend:

#2 Tuna Casserole

2 cups white sauce (see gravy/sauce section)
1 tsp. dry mustard
2-6-½ oz. can tuna
1 cup chopped black olives
1 cup whole kernel corn, drained
1 cup cooked wheat berries
Salt and pepper to taste

Blend mustard into white sauce. Add remaining ingredients and bake in a casserole dish for 40 minutes at 350 degrees. Top with biscuits, cornflakes or breadcrumbs

236

Main Dish Corner

Tuna or Chicken Filling
for Crepes

A topping for Pastas, Rice or Crepes

3 cups cooked diced chicken <u>or</u> tuna
¼ cup butter <u>or</u> margarine
1 medium onion, chopped
2 Tbsp. capers (optional)
4 tsp. chicken bouillon
6 cups boiling water
1-cup evaporated milk
1-cup creamy soup base <u>or</u> ½ cup white flour
¼ cup mushrooms (optional)
½ - 1 cup broccoli <u>or</u> asparagus (precooked)
¼ tsp. pepper
2 Tbsp. lemon juice
1 tsp. salt
½ cup Parmesan Cheese

Prepare chicken either a fryer, frozen breasts, or canned; or canned tuna, drained.
Sauté onions in butter a few minutes. Add capers and sauté another minute. Dissolve chicken bouillon in the boiling water mixture, and then add to the onion mixture. Simmer about 10 minutes. Mix together creamy soup base or flour with evaporated milk and pour into boiling chicken broth. (It mixes great in a blender.) Cook until thickened. Add salt, pepper, lemon juice and Parmesan cheese. Mix chicken <u>or</u> tuna and vegetables into sauce and serve over pasta, rice or rolled up in crepes. **YUMMY!**

Main Dish Corner

Turkey Casserole

3 cups cooked whole-wheat berries
2 cups cooked cubed turkey or chicken
¼ cup butter or margarine
¼ cup onion, chopped
½ cup celery, chopped   *Yummy*
2 cups broccoli, fresh or frozen
¼ cup all purpose flour in ¼ cup cold water
2 cups chicken broth or 2 tsp chicken bouillon diluted in
2 cups hot water
1-cup milk
1 tsp. salt
Pepper to taste
1 tsp. Accent
1 tsp. poultry seasoning
1 cup mild cheddar cheese, grated
½ cup slivered almonds (optional)
Breadcrumbs (optional)

Melt butter, add onion and celery. Cook until tender.
Blend in flour/water mixture. Stir in chicken broth and
milk. Add broccoli. Cook over low heat, stirring
constantly until thickened. Add seasonings, wheat,
turkey and cheese. Pour into buttered, 2 qt. casserole
dish. Sprinkle with almonds and more cheese or
breadcrumbs. Bake at 350 degrees for 30 – 40 minutes.

Serves 6

Main Dish Corner

Turkey Pilaf

Use your leftover turkey for this meal.

2 cups cooked, leftover turkey, chopped
2 cups cooked wheat berries
¼ cup butter <u>or</u> margarine
½ cup onion, chopped
½ tsp. celery seeds
½ tsp. ground thyme
2 tsp. dried leaf parsley
½ cup hot water
2 chicken bouillon cubes <u>or</u> 2 tsp. Knorr's chicken granules.
1-16 oz. can diced tomatoes, drained
1/3 cup raisins <u>or</u> chopped mixed dried fruits
¼ cup walnuts, chopped <u>or</u> pecans (optional)

In a large skillet or saucepan, melt butter. Stir in onion and sauté 2 minutes. Mix in turkey, celery seeds, thyme and parsley. Cook and stir about 5 minutes until turkey is lightly browned. In a small bowl, pour hot water over bouillon cubes. Stir to dissolve. Add bouillon mixture, wheat, tomatoes and raisins into turkey mixture. Add walnuts or pecans (optional). Cover and bring to a boil. Simmer over medium-low heat for 15 – 20 minutes. Serve immediately.

Serves 5 - 6

Wheat and Hamburger Casserole

2 cups whole wheat berries, cooked
4 cups water
1 lb. hamburger
1-cup onion, chopped
½ cup green pepper, chopped
1 tsp. chili powder
1 tsp. garlic powder
1 clove garlic, minced
1 tsp cumin or oregano
1 qt. jar tomatoes or 2-16 oz. cans diced tomatoes
2-8 oz. cans tomato sauce
1 sm. can chopped olives
2 cups grated Jack cheese

Brown hamburger with onions and green peppers in large skillet. Add wheat along with spices. Stir in tomatoes, sauce, and olives. Simmer for 30 minutes. Place in an oven proof casserole dish, top with cheese and bake at 350 degrees for 30 minutes.

Serves 8

WHEAT,
OUR POT OF
AMERICAN
GOLD !

Main Dish Corner

Wheat Ball Stroganoff

2 ½ cups cooked cracked wheat
2 eggs
½ cup milk
3 Tbsp. onions, minced
¼ tsp. nutmeg
1 ½ tsp. salt
¼ tsp. Worcestershire sauce
1 cup all-purpose flour
1 tsp. garlic powder
1 tsp. onion powder
Salt/pepper to taste
Vegetable oil
2 cups beef broth, thickened with a flour/water paste

Mix first 7 ingredients together and form into balls. Roll in flour, seasoned with garlic and onion powder, salt and pepper. Brown in large skillet in vegetable oil.
Thicken beef broth to desired consistency (like a thick gravy). Add meatballs. Simmer 5 minutes. Turn off heat and add ½ - 1 cup sour cream to broth.

Serve over noodles, rice or potatoes.

Yield: 70 balls

Main Dish Corner

Wheat Casserole

1 lb. ground beef <u>or</u> substitute
1-cup whole-wheat berries (soaked overnight)
1 onion, diced
2 cans tomato soup
½ cup catsup or tomato sauce
1 clove garlic, minced
1 Tbsp. parsley flakes
1 tsp. celery flakes
Salt/pepper to taste
Cheddar cheese, grated

Drain soaked wheat, add more water and simmer gently
for one hour. In a large skillet, brown ground beef,
onions and seasonings. Drain wheat again. Combine
wheat, meat mixture, soup and catsup in casserole dish.
Add water, if necessary. Sprinkle with cheese, and bake
at 350 degrees for 30 minutes.

WHEAT, OUR POT OF AMERICAN GOLD !

Main Dish Corner

Wheat Chili

2 cups cooked wheat berries
2 lbs. ground beef <u>or</u> TVP granules <u>or</u> half and half
1 large onion – minced
½ cup green pepper – diced
1-2 Tbsp. chili powder
1 tsp. garlic powder
1 tsp. oregano
2 cans tomato sauce
1 cup stewed tomatoes

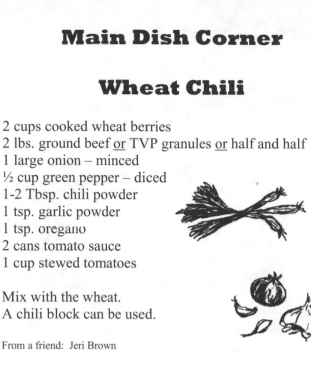

Mix with the wheat.
A chili block can be used.

From a friend: Jeri Brown

**WHEAT,
OUR POT OF
AMERICAN
GOLD !**

243

Main Dish Corner

Wheat Chili

More cracked wheat Chili, that's thick, hearty & packed with flavor.

1 lb. ground beef, browned and drained
2 medium onions, chopped
1 cup celery, chopped (optional)
1 cup green pepper, chopped
2 cloves garlic, minced
2 Tbsp. olive oil
1 Tbsp. chili powder
1 tsp. cumin
1 tsp. dried basil
1 qt jar canned tomatoes, undrained <u>or</u> 2 - 16 oz. cans diced tomatoes, undrained
1- 8 oz. can tomato sauce
1 tsp. salt
½ cup ketchup
6 cups cracked wheat, cooked
1 – 1 ½ cups water
2 cans kidney beans, drained (optional)
Mild cheddar cheese
Cottage cheese (optional)

Sauté onions, celery, and green pepper in olive oil until tender. Add tomatoes and tomato sauce, spices, and ketchup. Add meat if desired. Cook for 20 minutes to blend flavors. Add cracked wheat and cook 30 minutes, stirring occasionally. If desired add kidney beans.

Top with grated mild cheddar cheese and a scoop of cottage cheese.

Main Dish Corner

Wheat Meat

2 cups wheat berries
1 cup raw sunflower seeds   *Yummy*
½ medium onion
1 tsp. Bernard Jensen protein seasoning (find at health food store)
OR: season to taste with sage, thyme, spike, or soy sauce
Olive oil

Put wheat berries in ½ gallon thermos and fill to the top with cold water. Soak overnight. Next day, pour water out. Pour boiling water over wheat filling to top of thermos. Screw lid on tight and let sit all day. This is called low heat cooking. This method retains nutrients in the wheat. **Or:**
Place wheat berries in large pot and cover with water. Bring water to boil, then turn down on low. Simmer for several hours until soft. Put wheat in a colander to drain. Put 2 cups cooked wheat berries in food processor. Add ½ cup sunflower seeds. Add ½ onion. Add protein seasoning to taste. Start out with 1 tsp., add more if desired. (The seasoning is very lumpy, so dissolve in small amount of hot water if necessary.) Repeat for the other half of wheat. Form into large or small patties and fry in pan with olive oil till brown. You may also form into meatballs.

From a dear friend: Billy Dawn Lohman (her homemade recipe)

Suggestions for eating Wheat Meat are:
Try your favorite salad dressing as a topping.
Make into balls and use with spaghetti sauce
Add cooked chunks to tossed salad
Add cooked wheat meat with already stir-fried veggies
Add to omelet
Use instead of hamburger in corn tortillas for tacos
Try a patty with fresh tomatoes and mayonnaise

Main Dish Corner

Wheat Patties

2 cups cooked cracked wheat
½ cup onion, chopped
1 tsp. soda
1/3-cup milk
2 eggs, beaten
½ cup fresh mint or parsley
Salt/pepper to taste
Garlic salt (optional)
½ cup oatmeal (optional)

Mix all above ingredients together, flatten into patties
and fry in a hot skillet with olive oil. Browning each
side till done.

From a friend:

WHEAT,
OUR POT OF
AMERICAN
GOLD !

Main Dish Corner

Wheat Sprout Patties

2 cups wheat sprouts *
1 egg, slightly beaten
2 Tbsp. onion, minced
2 Tbsp. green pepper, minced
2 Tbsp. mushrooms, chopped
2 Tbsp. carrots, shredded
Butter or oil
Season to taste

Grind wheat sprouts and shredded carrots in food processor; add egg and the rest of the vegetables. Mix well. Form into patties. In a skillet, heat butter or olive oil and add patties that are no more than ½ inch thick. Cook for a few minutes on each side over medium heat until browned. Sprinkle with seasonings. (Celery salt, garlic salt, onion salt, Accent, etc.)

*See SPROUTING section in the front of the book for detailed information on sprouting seeds.

Main Dish Corner

Whole Wheat Crepes

Heavier batter for dinner meals:

2 cups milk
1 cup whole-wheat flour
A pinch of salt
2 eggs
1 Tbsp. butter or margarine

**WHEAT,
OUR POT OF
AMERICAN
GOLD !**

Sift together flour & salt into bowl. Make a well in the
center of flour and add eggs. Pour in half of the milk,
stirring constantly. Stir in melted butter or margarine.
Beat well, until smooth.

Add remaining milk, cover and let stand at room
temperature for at least 30 minutes before cooking. The
batter will thicken as it stands. If batter is too thick, add
a little more milk.

Heat crepe or omelet pan over medium heat. Add a little
oil or butter and roll around on pan so as to coat the
surface. Add batter and cook over medium high heat
until crepe is light brown. Turn quickly and cook other
side.
These crepes can be made ahead of time and refrigerated
or they can also be frozen. Use wax paper or plastic
wrap between each crepe and place in freezer bags
before freezing.

Find these wonderful fillings in this
corner for the crepe recipe above:

Asparagus Filling
Mozzarella/Crouton Filling
Mushroom Filling
Parmesan/Potato Filling
Tuna or Chicken Filling

Main Dish Corner

Whole Wheat Meat Loaf

1 ½ lbs. ground beef
¾ to 1 cup cooked whole kernel wheat
2 eggs
1 cup milk
¼ cup chopped onion
2 ½ tsp. salt
¼ tsp. pepper
1/3 tsp. sage
1 tsp. Worcestershire sauce
1 tsp. prepared mustard

Beat eggs in mixing bowl, add milk, then all other ingredients. Combine thoroughly and pack firmly in loaf tin. Bake at 350 degrees.

From a friend: Jeri Brown

Main Dish Corner

Whole Wheat Tamale Pie

¾ cup uncooked cracked wheat
1 ½ cup boiling water
2 8 oz. cans tomato sauce
2 lbs. ground beef
1 large onion, chopped
½ bell pepper, chopped
1 can black olives, drained and sliced
1/8 tsp. garlic salt
2 tsp. salt
1 tsp. coarse ground pepper
1 12 oz. or 16 oz. can whole kernel corn, drained
½ cup grated cheddar cheese

Cook wheat in water until thickened and all the water is absorbed. Be careful not to scorch. Add tomato sauce and set aside. Brown the beef, onion and bell pepper, drain off grease. Add salt, pepper and garlic. Combine beef mixture with olives, corn and tomato-wheat mixture, mix well and pack into a 11 x 9 inch pan and bake at 350 degrees for 45 minutes. After you remove from the oven sprinkle on the cheese before serving.

Serves 8

From a friend: Sandy Phelps

Main Dish Corner

Gravies & Sauces

Pan Gravy

2 Tbsp. vegetable oil or pan drippings
2 Tbsp. whole-wheat flour
1-cup cold liquid (may use the liquid drained from
wheat, veggies, or meat stock; or reconstituted bouillon)

Heat vegetable oil or drippings; add flour to cold liquid
and whip, shake, or beat until lumps are removed then
add to drippings, stirring constantly. Cook over
medium heat until smooth and thickened, stirring
constantly. You may need to add more flour paste to
make it thicker. Make sure you use cold liquid. Season
to taste with salt/pepper, garlic salt, Accent, etc.

Mushroom Gravy

2 Tbsp. sesame oil or olive oil
1-cup whole-wheat flour
2 medium onions, minced
¾ cup soy, tamari, or shoyu sauce
6 cups mushrooms, sliced
6 to 7 cups water

Heat oil and sauté onions and mushrooms. Mix flour
and soy sauce with water. Then add to above mixture.
Bring to boil over high heat, stirring often, then
simmer uncovered over medium heat for ½ hour,
stirring occasionally. Season to taste using beef or
chicken bouillon, salt/pepper, garlic salt, etc.

Main Dish Corner

Gravies & Sauces

Brown Roux

This sauce is used for thickening brown sauces; this paste may be made in advance and stored in refrigerator until needed.

Melt 1 cup butter <u>or</u> other fat in a heavy skillet; blend in 1 cup all-purpose flour to form a smooth paste. Stir and cook over low heat until mixture is light brown and roux is thoroughly cooked.

White Sauces

Foremost among basic sauces is white sauce. This is the indispensable base for innumerable sauces and is frequently used in other food preparation as well – in cream soups, casserole dishes, croquettes, and soufflés. White sauce as the name implies, is made with milk or cream. Spices, seasonings, and condiments add their piquant flavor to many variations of white sauce.

Medium White Sauce (Cream Sauce)

2 Tbsp. butter <u>or</u> margarine	1/8 tsp. pepper
2 Tbsp. flour	1 cup milk (use cream
½ tsp. salt	for richer sauce)

1. Heat butter in a saucepan. Blend in flour, salt and pepper; heat and stir until bubbly.
2. Gradually add the milk, stirring until smooth. Bring to boiling; cook and stir 1 to 2 minutes longer. Makes 1 cup

White Sauces – continued
Note: Add processed American cheese to this white sauce recipe to make a quick & easy cheese sauce.

Main Dish Corner

Gravies & Sauces

Thick White Sauce

Follow recipe for Medium White Sauce. Use 3 to 4
Tbsp. flour and 3 to 4 Tbsp. butter. Use in preparation
of soufflés and croquettes.

Thin White Sauce

Follow recipe for Medium White Sauce. Use 1 Tbsp.
flour and 1 Tbsp. butter. Use as a base for cream soups.

Normandy Sauce

The flavor of almost any vegetable may be enhanced
with this sauce. Use with these – celery, carrots,
cauliflower, asparagus or green peas.

Follow recipe for Medium White Sauce using 1½ times
the recipe. Substitute ½ cup light cream and 1 cup cider
for milk. Blend in ¼ tsp. lemon juice and ½ tsp. ground
nutmeg.

Normandy Cheese Sauce

2 Tbsp. flour	2 Tbsp. butter or
¼ tsp. salt	margarine
1/8 tsp. pepper	1 can (14½ oz.)
1 tsp. Worcestershire Sauce	evaporated milk
1 Tbsp. prepared mustard	½ cup water
¼ lb. processed American cheese	

1. Blend flour, salt/pepper, Worcestershire sauce, and
mustard with heated butter in a heavy saucepan; stir in
evaporated milk and water. Cook and

Continued…

Main Dish Corner

Gravies & Sauces

stir over low heat until thickened and smooth.

2. Add cheese and stir until melted.

Makes 2½ cups

Hollandaise Sauce

This rich sauce is used to enhance many foods, cooked green veggies, chicken and turkey, egg dishes, and others.

2 egg yokes
2 Tbsp. cream
¼ tsp. salt
A few grains cayenne pepper

2 Tbsp. lemon juice
or tarragon vinegar
½ cup butter

1. In the top of a double boiler, beat egg yolks, cream, salt, and cayenne pepper until thick with a whisk beater. Set over hot (not boiling) water. (Bottom of double boiler top should not touch water).
2. Add the lemon juice gradually, while beating constantly. Cook, beating constantly with the whisk beater, until sauce is the consistency of thick cream. Remove double boiler from heat, leaving top in place.
3. Beating constantly, add the butter, ½ tsp. at a time. Beat with whisk beater until butter is melted and thoroughly blended in.

About 1 cup

Continued…

Main Dish Corner

Gravies & Sauces

Note: The sauce may be kept hot 15 to 30 minutes over hot water. Keep covered and stir sauce occasionally.

Béarnaise Sauce

Follow recipe for Hollandaise Sauce. Add 1 peppercorn, crushed with the salt. Blend in, after the butter, 3 Tbsp. finely chopped fresh herbs such as tarragon, chervil, shallot (or green onion or chives), and parsley.

Brown Gravy

Method #1

3 Tbsp. fat	2 cups liquid, warm
3 Tbsp. flour	or cool (water; drip-
½ tsp. salt	pings; meat, chicken,
1/8 tsp. pepper	or vegetable broth; or
	milk

1. Add the fat to roasting pan (with brown drippings); stir in the flour and seasonings until smooth. Heat until bubbly. Brown slightly if desired.
2. Stir in the liquid and cook until sauce thickens; continue stirring and cooking 2 or 3 minutes longer, scraping bottom and sides of roasting pan to blend in the brown drippings or residue.

Makes about 2 cups gravy

Continued…

Main Dish Corner

Gravies & Sauces

Method #2

2 cups chicken or meat broth   ¼ cup flour
½ cup cold broth <u>or</u> water   ½ tsp. salt
                                    1/8 tsp. pepper

1. Bring the broth to boiling in a saucepan.
   Drippings from roasted meat or poultry may be
   substituted for part of the broth. If necessary,
   add milk <u>or</u> water to drippings to make 2 cups of
   liquid.
2. Measure broth and flour into a screw-top glass
   jar or shaker. Cover jar and shake until flour
   and broth are blended. Stirring boiling broth
   constantly, add flour mixture, a small amount at
   a time and bring to boiling after each addition.
   Cook and stir, adding only enough flour mixture
   until gravy is desired consistency. Add
   seasonings to taste. When gravy is thickened,
   cook 2 to 3 minutes longer.

Makes 2½ cups gravy

**WHEAT,
OUR POT OF
AMERICAN
GOLD !**

Muffins & Sweet
Breads Corner

Muffins & Sweet Bread Corner

Applesauce and Carrot Muffins

½ cup hot water
½ cup raisins
1-cup all-purpose flour
¾ cup whole-wheat flour
1 tsp. baking soda
½ tsp. salt
1½ tsp. cinnamon
½ tsp. nutmeg

1/3 cup vegetable oil
1 egg
½ cup sugar
½ tsp. vanilla
¼ tsp. lemon extract
1 cup applesauce
¾ cup grated carrots

Preheat oven to 400 degrees

Pour hot water over raisins and let soak. Stir together flours, soda, salt and spices in a large bowl. In small bowl, using an electric mixer, beat egg and sugar until fluffy. Beat in oil, vanilla and lemon extracts and stir in applesauce. Add to flour mixture and stir just until blended. Fold in grated carrots and raisins (with water) Spoon into greased or paper-lined muffin tins. Bake for 15 to 18 minutes until lightly brown and a toothpick inserted into muffin comes out clean.

Makes 12 muffins.

From a friend:

Cinnamon Rolls

2 Tbsp. dry yeast
½ cup warm water
2 cups scalded milk
½ cup sugar
2 tsp. salt
½ cup shortening
4 cups flour – 2 cups whole wheat, 2 cups all-purpose
2 eggs

4 Tbsp. butter or marg.
1-cup sugar and 4 Tbsp. cinnamon mixed well

In small bowl sprinkle yeast over warm water. Set aside. In large mixing bowl, stir together scalded milk, sugar, salt and shortening. Let cool 4 minutes. Gradually add in 3½ cups of flour and yeast, mix with hands until dough begins to leave sides of bowl. Turn out onto a floured surface and knead until dough is smooth and elastic. You may need to add a little more flour if dough is too sticky. Place in lightly oiled bowl, turning to coat all of dough. Cover with damp towel and let rise in warm place until doubled. Punch down, turnover, and let rise again to almost double.

Divide in half and roll each half into a 9" by 18" rectangle. Spread each with 2 Tbsp. soft butter and sprinkle each with half of sugar mixture. Roll up tightly, beginning at wide side. Pinch edges of roll to seal. Cut into 1-inch slices and place in a greased 9" by 13" cake pan. Cover and let rise until doubled. Bake at 350 degrees for 25 to 30 minutes.

<u>Glaze</u>: Mix powdered sugar, milk and vanilla to a syrup like consistency and drizzle on top of warm rolls.

From a friend:

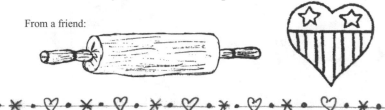

260

Muffins & Sweet Bread Corner

Easy Wheat Muffins

1½ cups whole wheat pastry flour
1½ cups baking powder
½ tsp. cinnamon
½ tsp. salt
2 Tbsp. powder milk
1 cgg
3 Tbsp. shortening
3 Tbsp. honey
¾ cup water

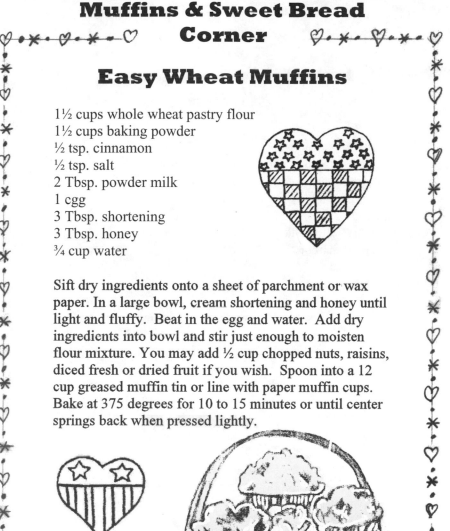

Sift dry ingredients onto a sheet of parchment or wax paper. In a large bowl, cream shortening and honey until light and fluffy. Beat in the egg and water. Add dry ingredients into bowl and stir just enough to moisten flour mixture. You may add ½ cup chopped nuts, raisins, diced fresh or dried fruit if you wish. Spoon into a 12 cup greased muffin tin or line with paper muffin cups. Bake at 375 degrees for 10 to 15 minutes or until center springs back when pressed lightly.

Muffins & Sweet Bread Corner

Fabulous and Hearty Muffins

2 quarts boiling water
2 cups quick oats
2 cups sugar
1 cup vegetable oil
4 eggs beaten
1 quart buttermilk
1 tsp. cinnamon

3 cups whole-wheat flour
2 cups all-purpose flour
5 tsp. baking soda
1 tsp. salt
4 cups all bran cereal
1 cup chopped nuts
1 cup raisins or chopped dates

Preheat oven to 375 degrees

Pour boiling water into a very large mixing bowl, add the oats and let cool. Mix together sugar, oil, eggs and buttermilk and stir into the oat mixture. Sift together dry ingredients. Add sifted dry ingredients and all bran cereal to oat mixture. Add cinnamon, fruit, and nuts. Combine well. Grease or paper line muffin tins and fill ¾ full with batter. Bake for 15 to 20 minutes or until the center springs back when lightly touched.

This recipe makes 5 dozen.

Fantastic Zucchini Bread

2 cups sugar
1-cup vegetable oil
2 eggs
2 tsp. vanilla
3 cups whole-wheat flour
1 tsp. cinnamon
½ tsp. nutmeg
1 tsp. salt
¼ tsp. baking powder
1 tsp. baking soda
2 cups shredded zucchini, unpeeled
1 cup chopped walnuts

Combine in large bowl, sugar, oil, eggs and vanilla. Mix well. Add dry ingredients and blend thoroughly. Fold in zucchini and nuts until well incorporated.

Pour Mixture into 2 greased and floured 4 1/2" by 8 1/2" bread pans and bake for 60 minutes at 350 degrees.

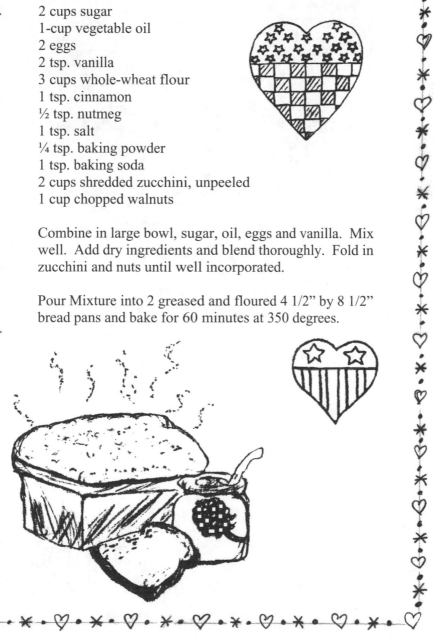

Glazed Orange Rolls

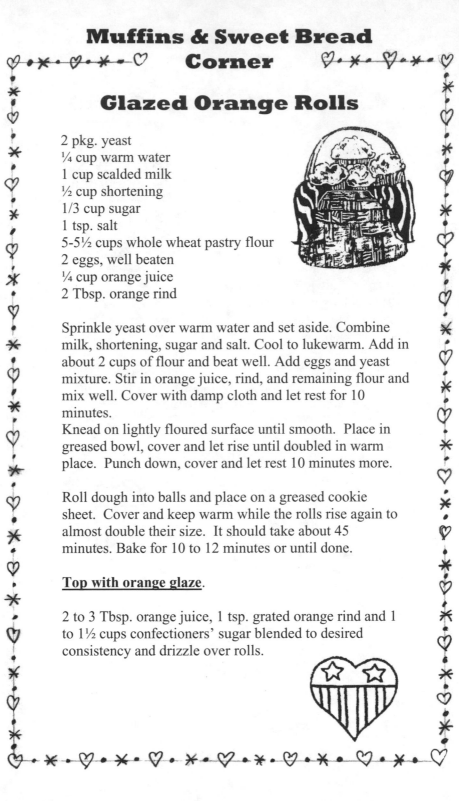

2 pkg. yeast
¼ cup warm water
1 cup scalded milk
½ cup shortening
1/3 cup sugar
1 tsp. salt
5-5½ cups whole wheat pastry flour
2 eggs, well beaten
¼ cup orange juice
2 Tbsp. orange rind

Sprinkle yeast over warm water and set aside. Combine milk, shortening, sugar and salt. Cool to lukewarm. Add in about 2 cups of flour and beat well. Add eggs and yeast mixture. Stir in orange juice, rind, and remaining flour and mix well. Cover with damp cloth and let rest for 10 minutes.
Knead on lightly floured surface until smooth. Place in greased bowl, cover and let rise until doubled in warm place. Punch down, cover and let rest 10 minutes more.

Roll dough into balls and place on a greased cookie sheet. Cover and keep warm while the rolls rise again to almost double their size. It should take about 45 minutes. Bake for 10 to 12 minutes or until done.

Top with orange glaze.

2 to 3 Tbsp. orange juice, 1 tsp. grated orange rind and 1 to 1½ cups confectioners' sugar blended to desired consistency and drizzle over rolls.

Muffins & Sweet Bread Corner

Old Fashioned Banana Nut Bread

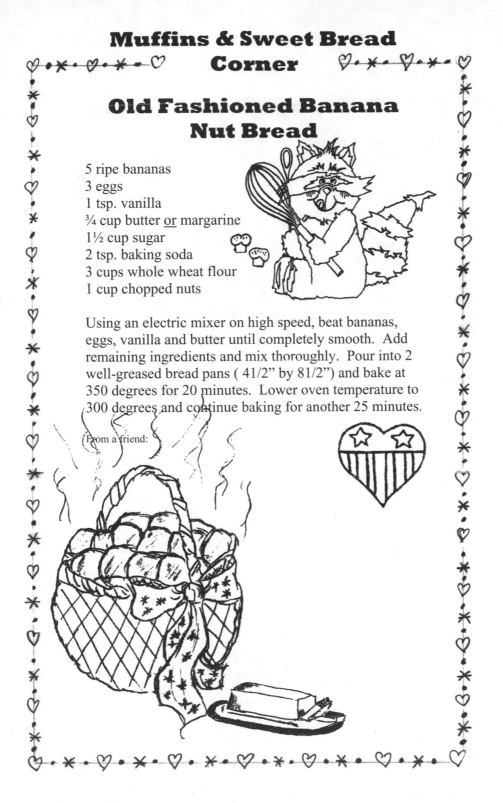

5 ripe bananas
3 eggs
1 tsp. vanilla
¾ cup butter <u>or</u> margarine
1½ cup sugar
2 tsp. baking soda
3 cups whole wheat flour
1 cup chopped nuts

Using an electric mixer on high speed, beat bananas, eggs, vanilla and butter until completely smooth. Add remaining ingredients and mix thoroughly. Pour into 2 well-greased bread pans (41/2" by 81/2") and bake at 350 degrees for 20 minutes. Lower oven temperature to 300 degrees and continue baking for another 25 minutes.

From a friend:

Orange Nut Bread

2 cups whole wheat flour
1 tsp. soda
1 tsp. baking powder
1 cup sugar
½ cup butter <u>or</u> margarine
2 eggs
Rind of one large orange, grated
1 cup sour milk
1 cup each of raisins and chopped nuts

Combine dry ingredients in bowl or onto parchment paper. In large mixing bowl, cream together sugar, butter, eggs and orange rind. Add sour milk and mix well. Add dry ingredients, raisins and nuts, blending in thoroughly.

Pour into greased and floured bread pan and bake for 1 hour at 325 degrees.

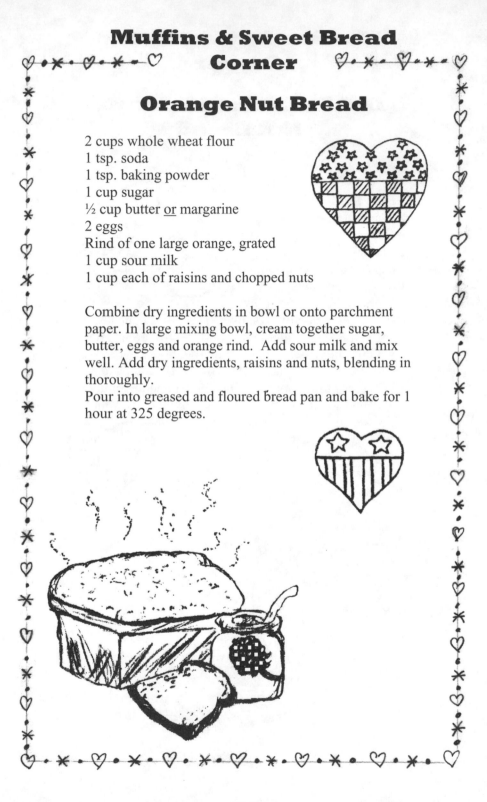

Muffins & Sweet Bread Corner

Pumpkin Bread

1¼ cups sugar
½ cup shortening
2 eggs
1 tsp. vanilla
1 cup pumpkin
¾ cup milk
1¾ cups whole wheat flour

¼ cup corn starch
½ tsp. salt
2 tsp. baking powder
1 tsp. cinnamon
½ tsp. nutmeg
½ tsp. ginger
½ cup nuts or raisins

Cream together sugar, shortening, eggs and vanilla in a large mixing bowl. Combine pumpkin and milk in a small bowl. Sift dry ingredients and add to creamed mixture alternately with pumpkin mixture. Fold in nuts or raisins. (Optional)

Pour into greased and floured bread pan and bake at 350 degrees for 45 to 50 minutes.

Pumpkin Wheat Muffins

2-¾ cups sugar (I use brown sugar)

1 cup vegetable oil   1 tsp. baking powder

4 eggs   1 tsp. baking soda

2 cups pumpkin   1 tsp. salt

1 tsp. cinnamon   2/3 cup water

1 tsp. nutmeg   31/2 cups whole wheat

½ tsp. cloves   flour

Mix all ingredients in order. You may add raisins or nuts if desired. Spoon into prepared muffin tins and bake at 375 degrees for 15 to 20 minutes.

From a dear friend: Lisa Pantone

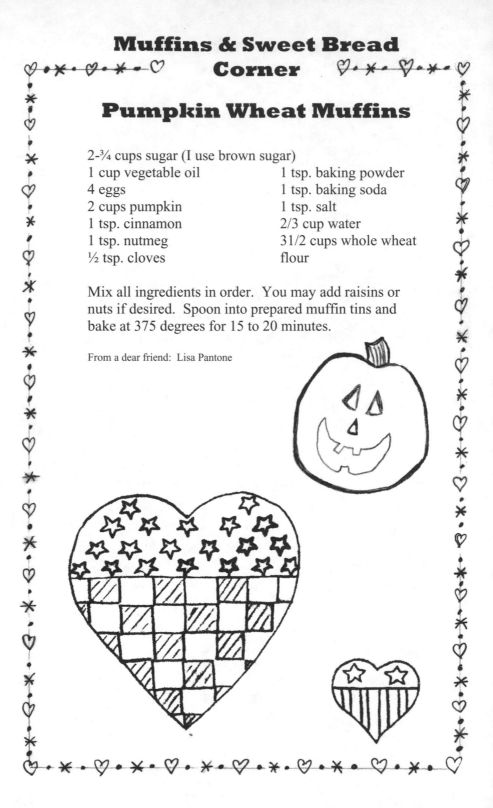

Muffins & Sweet Bread Corner

Some Fun Variations for our Whole Wheat Roll Recipe

No. 1
Pull-a-Part Breakfast Bread

1 cup sugar blended with 4 tsp. of cinnamon
½ cup melted butter
½ cup chopped pecans

Pinch off golf ball sized pieces of dough and roll in melted butter, then into sugar mixture. Arrange them in layers in an oiled angel food pan, sprinkling your pecans on top of each layer. Pan should be no more than 2/3 full. Let rise and bake for 45 minutes at 350 degrees. Remove immediately from pan and drizzle with glaze.

Glaze: 1 cup powdered sugar, 1 tsp. vanilla and enough milk to reach the desired consistency.

No. 2
Crescent Rolls

Roll out a circle of dough ½ inch thick and 12 inches in diameter. Cut into desired sized pie shaped pieces. Rolling from the wide end to the point, placing on greased cookie sheet, point placed underneath. Bake at 350 degrees for 18 to 20 minutes. You may brush with melted butter immediately out of oven if you so desire.

Wheat Berry Muffins

½ cup sugar, honey or molasses
2 Tbsp. shortening
1 egg, well beaten
1 cup cooked wheat berries
¾ cup milk
1 cup whole wheat or all-purpose flour (may use ½ & ½)
2½ tsp. baking powder
½ tsp. salt

Cream together sugar, honey or molasses with shortening. Add egg and mix well. Put wheat berries and milk into blender and blend until smooth. Combine sugar and milk mixtures. Sift dry ingredients and stir into milk mixture. Fill 12 greased muffin cups 2/3 full and bake for 25 to 30 minutes at 400 degrees.

Whole Wheat Doughnuts

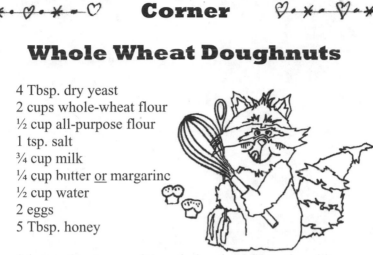

4 Tbsp. dry yeast
2 cups whole-wheat flour
½ cup all-purpose flour
1 tsp. salt
¾ cup milk
¼ cup butter <u>or</u> margarine
½ cup water
2 eggs
5 Tbsp. honey

Stir together 1-cup of the whole-wheat flour, the white flour and yeast in a large mixing bowl. Warm milk, butter and water to 130 degrees. Add to dry ingredients in bowl and mix thoroughly. Add the remaining whole-wheat flour, salt, eggs and honey and blend in completely.

Turn out onto a floured surface and knead for 5 to 7 minutes. Dough should be smooth and not sticky. Roll out to ½ " thickness. Cut with doughnut cutter and allow to rise. Deep fry in hot oil at 365 degrees approximately 1½ minutes per side. Drain on paper towels and dip in cinnamon and sugar or powdered sugar.

To glaze, (recipe below) string doughnuts on a wooden spoon or dowel and place over bowl. Pour glaze over doughnuts and transfer to plate.

<u>Glaze</u>: 4 cups sifted powder sugar, 1/3-cup milk and 1 tsp. vanilla, almond or orange extract. Mix until well blended.

Soup & Salad Corner

Apples and Wheat Berry Salad

3 cups cooked wheat berries
1 cup diced celery
2 large red apples, cored and diced
1 cup raisins
¾ cup mayonnaise
3 Tbsp. sugar
1 ½ tsp. fresh lemon juice
½ tsp. nutmeg

Combine all ingredients in a large bowl and mix well. Refrigerate for 2 to 3 hours. To serve, place on a bed of lettuce and sprinkle with chopped walnuts or grated cheddar cheese.

Makes 6 to 8 servings.

Asparagus and Wheat
Berry Vinaigrette

1 pkg. herb-flavored oil and vinegar salad dressing mix
Tarragon-flavored white wine vinegar
Vegetable <u>or</u> olive oil
2 Tbsp. chopped fresh parsley
1 Tbsp. finely chopped chives
2 tsp. capers
¼ cup cooked wheat berries
36 spears asparagus, cooked and chilled

Prepare salad dressing mix as directed using tarragon-flavored vinegar and your choice of oil. Mix parsley, chives, capers and wheat berries with 1 cup of prepared dressing. Chill for 1 hour. Place chilled asparagus on serving platter lined with Boston lettuce. Pour dressing over asparagus and garnish with thinly sliced cucumbers if desired.

Serve with hot crusty sourdough bread and butter.

This recipe serves 6.

Soup & Salad Corner

Cabbage and Cracked Wheat Slaw

½ cup bulgur wheat
1 cup water
½ tsp. salt
2/3 cup mayonnaise
3 Tbsp. cider vinegar
2 ½ Tbsp. sugar
½ tsp. hot sauce
½ tsp. dill
½ tsp. Dijon mustard
½ cup thinly sliced green onion
1 ½ cups finely shredded cabbage
1/3 cup shredded carrots
½ cup thinly sliced celery

Combine wheat, water and salt in 2-qt. saucepan and bring to boil. Reduce heat, cover and simmer until liquid is absorbed. (About 15 minutes.) While wheat is cooking, combine mayonnaise, cider vinegar, sugar, hot sauce, mustard and green onions; blend well. Add mayonnaise mixture to hot cooked wheat and mix well. Cover and chill for several hours or overnight. About 1 hour before serving, combine cabbage, carrots, and celery with chilled wheat mixture. Salt and pepper to taste. Place slaw into a serving bowl and chill until ready to serve.

The cooked bulgur wheat gives a wonderful nutty flavor to this crunchy cabbage slaw.

Makes 6 servings.

Soup & Salad Corner

Carrot, Pineapple and Wheat Berry Salad

2 ½ cups shredded carrots
1 8-oz. can crushed pineapple, drained
2 cups cooked wheat berries
½ cup raisins
½ cup mayonnaise or salad dressing
1 tsp. honey

Combine all the ingredients and chill for at least 1 hour.
Serves 6 to 8.

Pineapple, Marshmallow and Wheat Berry Slaw

4 cups shredded green cabbage
1 ½ cups wheat berries
½ cup green bell pepper, diced
1-8 oz. can crushed pineapple, drained
¾ cup mayonnaise or salad dressing
½ cup sour cream
¼ cup milk
2 tsp. honey
1 1/2 to 2 cups miniature marshmallows

Combine all ingredients except the marshmallows. Mix
well. Fold in marshmallows and chill 1 to 2 hours before
serving.

Yummy

Serves 6 to 8.

Your children are sure to like these fun salads

From a dear friend: Sandy Phelps

Soup & Salad Corner

Cheese and Broccoli Ham Soup

½ cup chopped onion
3 Tbsp. butter
¼ cup whole wheat pastry flour
1 tsp. dry mustard
½ tsp. dried thyme, crushed
2 cups milk
2 cups canned chicken broth
2 cups broccoli flowerets _or_ frozen cut broccoli
1 ½ cup cubed fully cooked ham
1 cup grated cheddar cheese

In a 3 quart saucepan melt butter and cook onions until tender and transparent. Stir in flour, dry mustard and the thyme. Add milk and broth all at once and cook over medium heat until thick and bubbly, stirring constantly. Stir in the broccoli and ham and return to a boil. Reduce heat and simmer for 5 to 6 minutes or until broccoli is tender, stirring occasionally.
Add cheddar cheese and stir until melted.

Ladle into bowl and garnish with additional cheese.
This creamy soup goes great with warmed whole wheat bread and butter. (See bread corner.)

Makes 4 servings

Chicken, Corn & Cheese Chowder

3 slices bacon
½ cup chopped onion
2 cups canned chicken broth
1-10 oz. pkg. frozen corn
2 medium potatoes, peeled and diced
½ cup thinly sliced celery
¾ tsp. savory, crushed
2 cups milk
2 Tbsp. whole wheat pastry flour
2 cups chicken breast, cooked and diced
2 cups grated cheddar cheese

In a large saucepan cook bacon until crisp. Remove bacon from pan, reserving drippings. Crumble bacon and set aside. Cook onion in bacon drippings until tender but not brown. Stir in chicken broth, corn, potatoes, celery and savory. Salt and pepper to taste. Bring to boil, reduce heat and cover. Simmer until vegetables are tender. In a small bowl, combine milk and flour together until well blended. Add to vegetable mixture stirring constantly until thickened and bubbly. Stir in chicken and cheese and cook until cheese is melted.
Ladle into bowls and top with crumbled bacon.

Makes 6 servings.

From a dear friend.

Soup & Salad Corner

Eggs and Bacon Salad

1 head lettuce
4 green onions, thinly sliced
4 hard cooked eggs, chopped
½ lb. crispy fried bacon, crumbled
¾ cup garlic flavored croutons
2 cups cooked wheat berries
½ to ¾ cup of your favorite French dressing
Salt and Pepper

In a large bowl, tear lettuce into bite-size pieces. Add onions, eggs, bacon, croutons and wheat berries. Toss together and add the French dressing. Salt and pepper to taste.

This tasty salad should be served immediately to maintain its wonderful crunch. A great main dish to serve at your Sunday morning brunch. Just add some fresh fruit and your menu is complete.

Serves 6.

From a dear friend: Sandy Phelps

A Favorite !

Soup & Salad Corner

Egg and Wheat Deli Salad

2 cups cooked wheat berries
1 small red onion, diced
2 sweet pickles, diced
4 hard cooked eggs, chopped
¾ cup salad dressing or mayonnaise
2 tsp. mustard
Salt and pepper to taste

Combine all ingredients in a bowl and refrigerate for at least 3 hours before serving.
A great side dish to cold fried chicken. This salad is also perfect to stuff a tomato with on those hot summer days.

Makes 4 servings.

GOD BLESS AMERICA

Four Bean & Wheat Salad

1-14 oz. can garbanzo beans
1-14 oz. can cut green beans
1-14 oz. can pinto beans
1-14 oz. can red kidney beans
2 cups cooked wheat berries
1 cup chopped red onion
1 ½ cup diced celery
½ cup chopped green pepper

Drain the beans. Place drained beans, wheat berries and chopped veggies into a large bowl and lightly toss.

<u>Marinade</u>:
¾ cup cider vinegar
1/3 cup vegetable or canola oil
1 clove garlic, minced
1 ½ Tbsp. honey
Salt and pepper to taste

Combine above ingredients and gently stir into bean mixture. Refrigerate. This salad needs to marinate for 24 hours before serving.

Makes 8 servings.

Ham and Turkey Club Salad

2 cups cooked wheat berries
1 cup diced ham
1 cup diced turkey
2 sweet pickles, diced
2 stalks of celery, diced
1 large carrot, shredded
¼ cup green pepper. Diced
1 small red onion, diced
1 cup grated cheddar cheese
3 hard cooked eggs, chopped
1 cup salad dressing or mayonnaise
2 tsp. mustard
Salt and pepper to taste

Combine all ingredients in a large bowl and mix well. Chill for at least 1 to 2 hours. Serve on a bed of lettuce and garnish with tomato slices.

This recipe makes 6 to 8 servings.

From a dear friend: Sandy Phelps

Italian Sausage Soup

12 cups water
1 pkg. onion soup mix
1-14 ½ oz diced Italian style tomatoes
1-cup cracked wheat
3 carrots, sliced
3 potatoes, cubed
2 stalks celery, sliced thinly
1 onion, chopped
1 clove garlic, minced
2 Tbsp. Italian seasoning
Salt and pepper to taste
1 lb. Italian sausage, mild or hot
1 lb. ground beef
1-16 oz. can cut green beans
1-16 oz. can whole kernel corn
1 ½ cup frozen peas
1-8 oz. can tomato sauce

Pour water into a large soup pot. Add soup mix,
tomatoes, cracked wheat, carrots, potatoes, celery,
onions, garlic and seasonings. Bring to a boil and let
simmer until vegetables are tender. Meanwhile, brown
sausage and ground meat. Drain meat and add to the
soup pot. Add the four remaining ingredients and
simmer on low for 30 minutes.

Serve this hearty soup with a sprinkling of Parmesan
cheese and hot crusty bread sticks. (See bread corner.)

Serves 8 to 10.

Soup & Salad Corner

Lentil and Kielbasa Soup

1 1/3 cups lentils
3 cups water
4 cups chicken broth
2 carrots, sliced
2 stalks celery, thinly sliced
1 small onion, diced
1-14 ½ oz. can stewed tomatoes
1 tsp. basil leaves, crushed
1 tsp. marjoram leaves, crushed
1 tsp. kosher salt
½ tsp. coarsely ground pepper
½ lb. Kielbasa sausage, sliced in 1 inch coins

Rinse lentils and place in a large soup pot. Add all remaining ingredients, cover and bring to boil. Reduce heat and simmer for 2 hours or until lentils are done.

This hearty soup is great served in our sourdough bowls. (See our grandma's corner for recipe.)

Serves 4 to 6.

Soup & Salad Corner

Mandarin Oranges and Wheat Salad

1-cup bulgur wheat
2 cups water
1-11 oz. can mandarin oranges, drained
1/3 cup mayonnaise
2 Tbsp. orange juice
2 Tbsp. lemon juice
1 Tbsp. chopped fresh chives
1 tsp. sugar
1 ¾ tsp. salt

Combine wheat and water in a large pan. Bring to a boil, reduce heat, cover and simmer until all the liquid is absorbed. (About 15 minutes.) Remove lid, and let cool. Add oranges to cooled bulgur. (Reserve some orange sections for garnish) Chill for at least 1 hour. Combine remaining ingredients and mix well. Pour over chilled wheat and oranges and toss gently. Serve on a bed of lettuce and garnish with reserved oranges.

Great accompaniment to a Chinese stir-fry.

Makes 4 to 6 servings.

GOD BLESS AMERICA

Mexican Shrimp Salad

1 head of lettuce, torn into bite-size pieces
2 cups cooked wheat berries
1 cup diced celery
3 green onions, thinly sliced
2 tomatoes, chopped into bite-size pieces
1 10 oz. pkg. frozen peas
1 can pitted black olives, sliced
2 cans shrimp, drained
¾ salad dressing
½ cup sour cream
2 ½ tsp. chili powder or to taste

Mix salad dressing, sour cream and chili powder together and set aside. Combine all of the remaining ingredients in a large bowl. Pour salad dressing over salad and lightly toss together. Serve with tortilla chips

This salad can be as spicy as you like.

From a dear friend.

GOD BLESS AMERICA

Minestrone Beef Soup

2 to 3 cups left over roast or steak
2 Tbsp. olive oil
1 Tbsp. butter or margarine
1-cup onion, chopped
1 cup celery, thinly sliced
1 clove garlic, minced
5 cups water
1-14 ½ oz. can chicken broth
1-14 ½ oz. can Italian flavored diced tomatoes
¾ cup shredded cabbage
2 carrots, Sliced
1 ½ tsp. oregano
1 tsp. basil, crushed
½ tsp. thyme
1 cup frozen peas
½ cup wheat berries
1 cup canned kidney beans, drained.
1 cup sliced zucchini

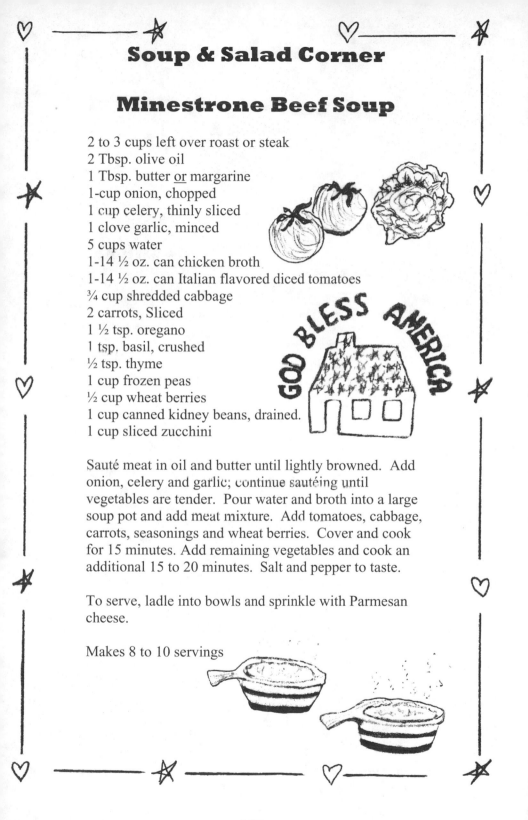

Sauté meat in oil and butter until lightly browned. Add onion, celery and garlic; continue sautéing until vegetables are tender. Pour water and broth into a large soup pot and add meat mixture. Add tomatoes, cabbage, carrots, seasonings and wheat berries. Cover and cook for 15 minutes. Add remaining vegetables and cook an additional 15 to 20 minutes. Salt and pepper to taste.

To serve, ladle into bowls and sprinkle with Parmesan cheese.

Makes 8 to 10 servings

Soup & Salad Corner

Peachy Chicken Oriental Salad

4 cups sliced peaches, drain and reserve juice
1 cup diced celery
2 cup cooked wheat berries
2 cups cooked chicken, diced
¾ cup mayonnaise or salad dressing
1 Tbsp. lemon juice
¼ cup peach juice
1 tsp. honey
1 can chow mein noodles

Combine all the ingredients except the noodles. Just before serving, toss with the noodles. Serve immediately. This is a great salad for those warm summer evenings.

Serves 6 to 8.

From a dear friend: Carla Thomas

Salad Provencal

2 green peppers, cut into strips
2 Tbsp. vegetable oil
3 large ripe tomatoes, cut into pieces
1 small Bermuda onion, sliced
½ lb. sliced mushrooms
1 small can whole pitted black olives
½ cup cooked wheat berries

Sauté peppers in oil until partially tender. Remove to bowl and add tomatoes, onion, mushrooms, olives and wheat berries.

Vinaigrette:

½ cup olive oil
¼ cup white wine vinegar
1 clove garlic, minced
Salt and pepper to taste

Combine above ingredients and mix well. Pour over salad and toss gently. Marinate at room temperature for 1 hour. Place in refrigerator for 30 minutes before serving.

Serves 6.

291

Sandy's Crab Salad

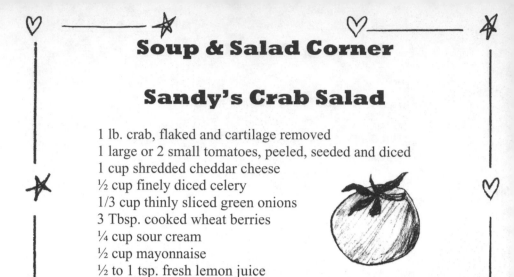

1 lb. crab, flaked and cartilage removed
1 large or 2 small tomatoes, peeled, seeded and diced
1 cup shredded cheddar cheese
½ cup finely diced celery
1/3 cup thinly sliced green onions
3 Tbsp. cooked wheat berries
¼ cup sour cream
½ cup mayonnaise
½ to 1 tsp. fresh lemon juice

Combine all ingredients in a medium sized mixing bowl. Cover and chill for several hours.

Place a scoop of crab salad on a bed of lettuce and garnish with tomato wedges. This salad makes a great sandwich served on a croissant or try stuffing a big ripe tomato with this delicious salad. **Yummy!**

Serves 4

From a dear friend: Sandy Phelps

A Favorite !

Tabbouleh
Wheat Garden Salad

1 cup uncooked bulgar
3 medium ripe tomatoes, finely chopped
1 cup finely chopped parsley
1 cup finely chopped green onions (tops & bottoms)
½ cup cubed cucumber (optional)
½ cup fresh lemon juice
2 tsp. salt
½ cup olive oil
2 Tbsp. fresh mint finely cut <u>or</u> 2 Tbsp. dried mint
May use basil in place of mint
Romaine lettuce (and the leaves)

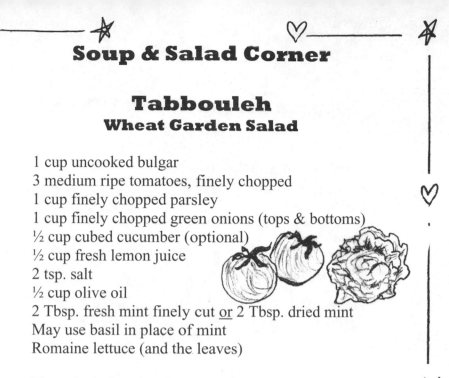

Place the bulgar in a bowl or pan and pour in enough cold water to cover it by several inches. Let it soak for about 30 minutes or until it has doubled in size. Squeeze out all excess water by squeezing handfuls of wheat and then placing it into a large salad bowl. Add the tomatoes, parsley, onions, and salt. Mix lemon and oil together and pour it over the salad. Toss thoroughly with a fork. Sprinkle on the mint and toss again. Serve immediately.
You may serve it with crisp romaine leaves and use them as scoops to eat with. This is the custom in the Middle East

Serves 4 - 6

From a friend: Sandy Phelps

Yummy

GOD BLESS AMERICA

Tuna and Cracked Wheat Salad

2 cups cooked cracked wheat
1-12 oz. or 2-6 oz. cans tuna, flaked
½ cup mayonnaise
¼ cup thinly sliced green onions
¾ cup diced celery
1/4 cup sliced black olives (Optional)
1 tsp. fresh lemon juice

Place all ingredients into a medium-mixing bowl and lightly toss together. This salad is best when chilled overnight. Serve on a bed of lettuce and garnish with a lemon slice.

Makes 4 to 6 servings.

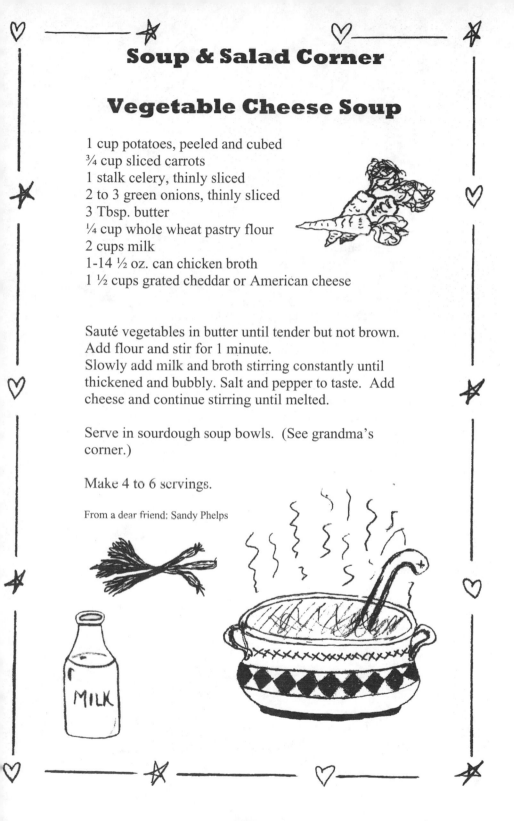

Soup & Salad Corner

Vegetable Cheese Soup

1 cup potatoes, peeled and cubed
¾ cup sliced carrots
1 stalk celery, thinly sliced
2 to 3 green onions, thinly sliced
3 Tbsp. butter
¼ cup whole wheat pastry flour
2 cups milk
1-14 ½ oz. can chicken broth
1 ½ cups grated cheddar or American cheese

Sauté vegetables in butter until tender but not brown.
Add flour and stir for 1 minute.
Slowly add milk and broth stirring constantly until
thickened and bubbly. Salt and pepper to taste. Add
cheese and continue stirring until melted.

Serve in sourdough soup bowls. (See grandma's
corner.)

Make 4 to 6 servings.

From a dear friend: Sandy Phelps

Wheat Berry Chef Salad

1 head iceberg lettuce, washed and torn into bite-size pieces
3 cups torn leaf lettuce or romaine
4 oz. fully cooked ham, cut into julienne pieces
4 oz. cooked breast of turkey, cut into julienne pieces
4 oz. julienne strips of Swiss or Monterey jack cheese
4 oz. julienne strips of Cheddar or American cheese
4 hard-cooked eggs cut in half lengthwise
2 medium tomatoes, each cut into 8 wedges or 8 cherry tomatoes, halved
1 small red or green pepper, cut into rings
1 small Bermuda onion, thinly sliced into rings
1 cup cooked wheat berries
1 cup of your favorite salad dressing

In a large bowl, toss together greens. Place ¼ of the greens onto 4 dinner plates. Arrange ¼ of the meats, cheeses, hard cooked eggs, tomatoes, peppers and onions over the green on each plate.
Sprinkle ¼ cup wheat berries on each salad. Pour ¼ cup dressing into 4 small serving dishes and serve with salads.

The wheat berries are a healthy change from croutons and add a wonderful nutty flavored crunch to this chef salad.

Makes 4 main-dish servings.

Soup & Salad Corner

Wheat Berry Chicken Pasta Salad

4 cups cooked chicken breast, cubed
2 cups diced Granny Smith green apple
8 ounces corkscrew pasta, cooked and drained
1-8 ½ oz. can pineapple chunks, drained
½ cup red seedless grapes, halved
1 stalk celery, thinly sliced
2 to 3 green onions, thinly sliced
½ cup cooked wheat berries

Combine all ingredients in a large bowl.

Dressing:
1 cup mayonnaise
1/3 cup plain yogurt
1 tsp. lime zest
3 Tbsp. lime juice
1 ½ Tbsp. honey
2 tsp. grated <u>fresh</u> ginger
¼ tsp. kosher salt

Combine all dressing ingredients together and gently stir into chicken mixture. Cover and chill for 3 to 4 hours to allow flavors to blend. Serve on a bed of green or red leaf lettuce.

This refreshing pasta salad goes well with wheat thin crackers. (See crackers and pastas corner.)

Makes 8 to 10 servings.

GOD BLESS AMERICA

Wheat Berry Mushroom Salad

3 cups cooked wheat berries
½ lb. thinly sliced mushrooms
1- 4 oz. can sliced black olives
¾ cup thinly sliced green onions
1 green bell pepper, sliced into rings for garnish

Combine wheat berries, mushrooms and olives. Add vinaigrette dressing and marinate for 2 hours or overnight. Stir in green onions. Serve in a lettuce leaf and garnish with bell pepper rings.

Vinaigrette Dressing:

Combine and mix well:

1/3 cup vegetable oil
1/3 cup white wine vinegar
1 glove garlic, minced
1 ½ tsp. oregano leaves, crushed
Salt and pepper to taste

This is a great low-fat salad and is very satisfying.

INDEX

BREAD & BISCUIT CORNER

BREAD MACHINE CORNER

BREAKFAST CORNER

CRACKERS & PASTAS CORNER

DESSERT CORNER

GRANDMA'S SOURDOUGH CORNER

KIDDIES CORNER

MAIN DISH CORNER

MUFFINS & SWEET BREADS CORNER

SOUP & SALAD CORNER

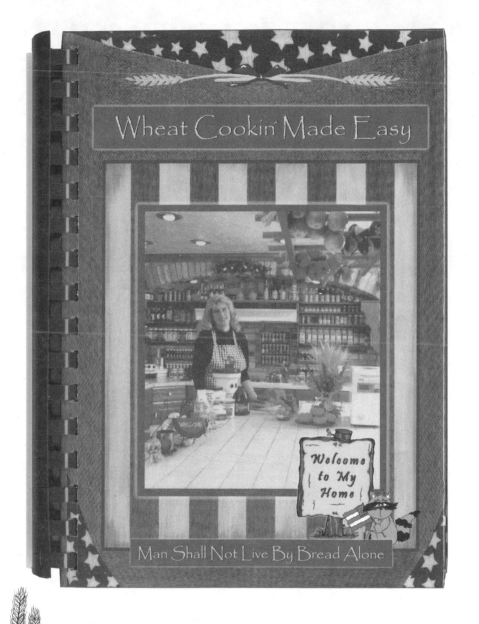

Wheat Cookin' Made Easy

Welcome
to My
Home

Man Shall Not Live By Bread Alone

IF YOU WOULD LIKE TO ORDER OUR

"WHEAT COOKIN' MADE EASY"

COOKBOOK, PLEASE SEE OUR WEBSITE AT

WWW.CROCKETTSCORNER.COM

WE ARE EXCITED TO ANNOUNCE OUR NEW PRODUCT LINE TO YOU, OUR FRIENDS. YOU MAY VIEW THESE ITEMS ON OUR WEBSITE AT WWW.CROCKETTSCORNER.COM

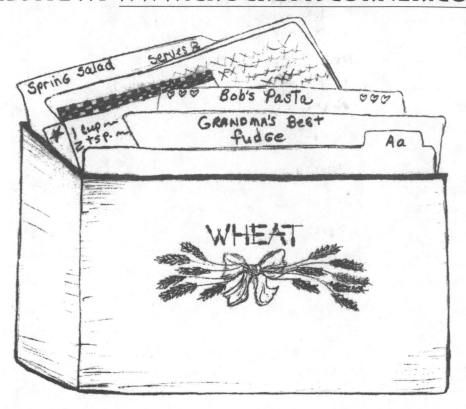

WE WOULD LIKE TO INVITE YOU TO SHARE YOUR FAVORITE FAMILY RECIPES WITH US. IF WE USE YOUR RECIPES, YOUR NAME WILL APPEAR IN OUR UPCOMING EDITIONS.

SANDY AND I ARE BUSY COMPILING RECIPES FOR THE FOLLOWING IDEAS: THE SQUASH FAMILY, SOUPS AND SALADS, MOMMY AND ME, WHOLE GRAIN COOKERY, MAIN DISHES, ETC.

ANY QUESTIONS ABOUT, OR IDEAS FOR UPCOMING EDITIONS, PLEASE EMAIL US AT CROCKFARM@NETWORLD.COM

DIMENSION 2000

HE NEW MILLENNIUM MIXER

UGGESTED RETAIL: **$249.95**

FETIME WARRANTY

HE TORNADO DRIVE BLENDER
ULVERIZES NUTS FOR NUT
UTTERS, BLENDS AWESOME
MOOTHIES WITH ITS
NIQUE FOLDING ACTION,
ND TURNS ICE INTO SNOW.

ASY TO USE TOUCH PANEL
NCLUDES THREE SPEEDS, PULSE
UTTON AND BREAD TIMER.

TTACHMENTS INCLUDE: WIRE WHISKS,
OUGH HOOK, MIXING BOWL, AND TORNADO
RIVE BLENDER. OTHER ATTACHMENTS SOLD SEPERATELY.

WHISPER MILL
NO HASSLE
LIFETIME WARRANTY

EASY TO USE AND CLEAN. MILLS 8 CUPS
OF GRAIN INTO 12 CUPS OF FLOUR IN
LESS THAN 2 MINUTES. WITH
MICROBURST TECHNOLOGY, THE
WHISPER MILL IS THE WORLD'S
QUIETEST, #1 FLOUR MILL.

SATISFACTION GARANTEED!
SUGGESTED RETAIL: **$199.95**

"SEAL IT™"

"SEAL IT"
CAN SEALING MACHINE

RY PACK CANS OF WHEAT, RICE, BEANS, DRY
OTATOES, POWDERED MILK, FLOUR, PASTA AND
AANY OTHER ITEMS FOR LONG TERM STORAGE.

NCLUDES:
GHTWEIGHT ALUMINUM CONSTRUCTION
OMMERCIAL STYLE HARDENED SEAMING ROLLERS FOR #10
ANS.
O VOLT HEAVYDUTY DIRECT-DRIVE GEAR MOTOR. NO
HAINS
TTACHED SCRATCH RESISTANT BASE PAD.
ABLE CLAMPS
AODEL A MOTOR-1/6 HP, 45 RPM. NOW AVAILABLE FOR
HE LOW INTRODUCTORY PRICE OF **$815.00**.
AODEL B MOTOR-1/4 HP, 70 RPM. **$949.00**.
PTIONAL ROLLER ADAPTER KITS FOR SEALING
300, #401 AND #404 CANS AVAILABLE. **$98.00**

ONE YEAR WARRANTY

ITEM PRICES DO NOT INCLUDE SHIPPING AND HANDLING COSTS.

WHEAT SPROUTS $5.95
ORGANIC SPROUTING SEEDS

LIVE AND SPROUTABLE RED OR WHITE WHEAT. MAY BE PURCHASED IN LARGER QUANTITIES AT A DISCOUNTED PRICE.

SUGGESTED RETAIL: **$12.95**

THE WORLD'S GREATEST SPROUTER AND CRISPER!

- REMOVEABLE DIVIDER
- STACKING CAPACITY
- EXCELLENT AIR CIRCULATION
- EASY TO USE
- MADE TO LAST
- ASSEMBLES QUICKLY
- EASY TO CLEAN

THE **SPROUTMASTER** IS PACKAGED AS ONE, TWO, OR THREE TRAYS THAT CAN BE STACKED OR USED SEPARATELY.

MARCATO GRAIN MILL
SUGGESTED RETAIL: $79.95

WHOLE GRAINS CAN EITHER BE ROLLED OR CRACKED WITH THIS MACHINE. THE MARCATO IS A HAND MILL WITH THREE STAINLESS STEEL ROLLERS AND THREE VARIABLE SETTINGS. EACH GRAIN OF SOFT GRAIN IS INDIVIDUALLY FLATTENED. HARD GRAIN CAN BE CRACKED FOR CEREAL. PUT THE GRAIN THROUGH TWO MORE TIMES FOR FLOUR.

MIRACLE WHEAT GRASS JUICER
SUGGESTED RETAIL: $69.95

EXTRACTS HEALTH-GIVING, VITAMIN-RICH JUICES FROM WHEAT GRASS, LEAFY VEGETABLES, SOFT FRUITS AND BERRIES.

ITEM PRICES DO NOT INCLUDE SHIPPING AND HANDLING COSTS